To my dear husband. Roger.

Valentin's day 2015

Love, Shahin

MANDELA

MANDELA

The Life of Nelson Mandela

ROD GREEN

Thomas Dunne Books
St. Martin's Press
New York

THOMAS DUNNE BOOKS.
An imprint of St. Martin's Press.

MANDELA. Text copyright © 2012 by Constable & Robinson.
Photographs copyright © Press Association Images (unless otherwise stated).
All rights reserved. For information, address St. Martin's Press, 175 Fifth Avenue,
New York, N.Y. 10010.

www.thomasdunnebooks.com
www.stmartins.com

Designed by Design 23, London

Printed in the United Kingdom by Butler Tanner & Dennis

All photographs supplied by Press Association Images except for those on the
following pages which were supplied courtesy of Rex Features 2, 25, 66, 68, 69, 77,
89, 98, 99, 107, 110, 112/13, 114, 119, 121, 122, 123, 144, 145, 146/147, 163, 164

Library of Congress Cataloging-in-Publication Data Available Upon Request

ISBN 978-1-250-05321-3 (hardcover)
ISBN 978-1-4668-5554-0 (e-book)

St. Martin's Press books may be purchased for educational, business, or promotional use.
For information on bulk purchases, please contact Macmillan Corporate and Premium Sales
Department at 1-800-221-7945, extension 5442, or write specialmarkets@macmillan.com.

Originally published in the United Kingdom by Constable,
an imprint of Constable & Robinson Ltd

First U.S. Edition

10 9 8 7 6 5 4 3 2 1

CONTENTS

INTRODUCTION

There can't be many people who have never heard the name Nelson Mandela. His has become a household name, a name respected by everyone everywhere, from grandmothers to schoolchildren. Not so many people would recognise his other names, and he is a man who has been known by several names throughout his life.

When he was on the run, with the ANC a banned organisation and Nelson one of its leaders, an arrest warrant hanging over his head, the South African press dubbed the elusive Mr Mandela 'The Black Pimpernel'.

It was an image that he, and others working with him, did everything they could to perpetuate in order to ensure that everyone inside and outside South Africa knew that the ANC was still, in those turbulent times in the early 1960s, pursuing their fight for freedom. But that manufactured image quickly became superfluous. Nelson's own name came to mean far more than any romanticised nickname.

What, however, does Nelson Mandela's real name actually mean? He was known by several names – Rolihlahla, the name given to him at birth; Nelson, the English name given to him when he first went to school; Dalibhunga, the name given to him when he went through his Xhosa tribal initiation ceremony; Madiba, the clan name used as a term of respect. To a certain degree the different names represent different periods in his life, and they certainly all have different meanings.

Rolihlahla translates into English as 'shaking the tree branch', which is a phrase taken to mean that anyone so named likes to cause a stir or is some kind of troublemaker. Nelson's parents could not have known how prophetic their choice of birth name was but, while his father died when Nelson was still a young boy, his mother was there to see Nelson live up to the name Rolihlahla.

Nelson was the name chosen for him by his schoolteacher, a traditional practice when African children first went to school. The teacher probably picked it on a whim, naming him after the English hero Horatio Lord Nelson. The actual name 'Nelson' means 'son of Neil' which you might not think at all significant to the life of the world's most famous freedom fighter, until you learn that the name Neil means 'champion'. Then, perhaps, the name suddenly seems a little more fitting.

Nelson's Xhosa initiation, or circumcision name, Dalibhunga, was most definitely a deliberate choice. The 'bhunga' in Dalibhunga is the name for a tribal council in the Transkei region where Nelson was brought up and the whole name is taken to mean 'convener' or 'founder' of the council, a name that reflects the role as adviser to the tribal chief which was once seen as Nelson's destiny. It was a role, after all, that his father had also fulfilled.

ABOVE: Nelson and Graça Machel leave Divinity School in Oxford following a Ceremony of Welcome, after which he was awarded the Freedom of the City.

The name Mandela, of course, has assumed a special meaning for people around the world. They associate Mandela with freedom, justice and equality. Mandela has become a symbol for civil rights, an icon of peace and the personification of wisdom. Mandela has become almost a religious figure, promoted to the level of sainthood by millions who would happily see him beatified, although, by his own admission, he falls well short of qualification for any form of canonization. He often said that he believed he had led a 'thoroughly immoral life', although he was always loath ever to elaborate on any details about his immorality. So what was he talking about?

There have been many rumours and allegations about him having had affairs during his first marriage, even hints at him having fathered an illegitimate child, but the towering events of his later life cast long and concealing shadows over such accusations. The public relations machine that created the accepted face of Nelson Mandela in order to keep the ANC cause and the fight for black emancipation in South Africa pricking the conscience of everyone who lived in freedom and comfort elsewhere in the world, was more than happy to leave his earlier life marooned in the past. Yet Nelson would never allow his failings to be swept completely under the carpet. 'I am not a saint,' he said, 'unless you think of a saint as a sinner who just keeps on trying.'

Later controversies that flared up around claims of financial irregularities, foreign bank accounts and alleged tax avoidance still could not leave even the slightest scorch mark on

Nelson's shining armour. The overwhelming fact is that he devoted his entire life to serving his people, not to helping himself. Had he wanted to, he could have made a very comfortable living in South Africa and become a relatively wealthy man by pursuing his career as a lawyer. Instead, he chose to go to jail, not once, but a number of times, culminating in 27 years of incarceration. Even while in prison, he chose to continue to work on behalf of his people, on behalf of his country, putting even the meagre comforts he was permitted in jail at risk. His life, in fact, could have been snuffed out by the

ABOVE: Canadian Prime Minister Jean Chretien presented Nelson with an Honorary Canadian Citizenship in Quebec in 2001.
RIGHT: Nelson with his daughter Zenani and granddaughter Ndileka in Johannesburg in 2011.

authorities in any number of different ways any number of times over the years. It takes a special kind of man to live with that knowledge dogging every step he ever takes. He did not, however, regard the hardships he endured as unique or outstanding. When revisiting his Robben Island prison cell some years after his release, Nelson told reporters that, 'There are many of my comrades who have sacrificed far more than I did.'

To continue to serve the people of South Africa after he was released from prison, at an age when most men would long since have settled down to a quiet retirement, placing, as he put it when addressing his supporters on his release, 'the remaining years of my life in your hands', shows the extraordinary dedication that truly set Nelson apart from his contemporaries. There were others who suffered as he did, others who served prison terms alongside him, but there were none who could play all of the parts that he did – lawyer, campaigner, politician, strategist, military commander, negotiator, diplomat, president, statesman.

The name Nelson Mandela would come to mean all of those things to millions of people all over the world and his immense achievements warrant him a place in history as one of the most influential men of the twentieth century.

CHAPTER ONE

Humble Beginnings

A boy who grew up in poverty, living in a house with no running water, no furniture, no proper sanitation and only mats to lie down on at night would not be judged to have had a privileged upbringing. That the boy had two sisters, three step-brothers and seven step-sisters, his father having had children with four separate partners, might also point to this being what is often referred to nowadays as a 'dysfunctional family'. You would not expect such a boy to grow up to become president of his country, a statesman of international renown and winner of the Nobel Peace Prize.

Nelson Mandela's humble beginnings, however, should not be judged by modern standards in what is termed 'the developed world'. His childhood in South Africa during the years between the First and Second World Wars was, in fact, far more conducive to the development of a healthy, well-adjusted youngster than the formative years of the majority of children in more prosperous European or American cities. The young Nelson, then known by the name his father had given him, Rolihlahla (usually taken to mean 'troublemaker'), was doted upon not just by his biological mother, Nosekeni Fanny, but by three others. 'I had

'There can be no keener revelation of a society's soul than the way in which it treats its children.'

NELSON MANDELA

mothers who were very supportive and regarded me as their son. Not as their step-son as you would say in the culture amongst whites,' he once said. 'They were mothers in the proper sense of the word.'

The home where Rolihlahla lived in the village of Qunu, nestling in the low hills of the Transkei region of South Africa's Eastern Cape Province, was a collection of round, mud-brick huts with grass roofs. In this rural community the boys tended to the livestock, mainly cattle, during the day while the girls and their mothers weeded the fields, collected water from the stream, looked after the home and prepared the food, mainly maize, for the meal that the family ate together in the evening. Many of the men were missing from their homes for much of the year, working on distant farms or labouring as miners, returning only to plough their fields perhaps only twice a year.

Mandela would later look back on this period of his childhood as the happiest time of his life. A shepherd and cowherd from the time he was five years old, he drank fresh milk straight from the cow, swam in pools and streams and wandered the hills, free as a bird. Like the other boys from his village, young Rolihlahla wore only a blanket slung over one shoulder and fastened around his waist. He learned 'stick fighting', brandishing a wooden staff just as it is used in various forms of martial arts around the world,

PREVIOUS SPREAD: The rolling hills of the Transkei region where Nelson spent his childhood.
LEFT: Villagers near Umtata, close to where Nelson was born, outside their traditional mud-brick homes.

and joined in with his friends when they challenged boys from other villages to games that involved throwing sticks and defending targets. Memories of that innocent freedom and outdoors life are what drew Mandela back to the area on his release from Victor Verster prison in 1990. He built a modest house on a family plot near Qunu.

Mandela's early years (he was born on 18 July 1918) were not, however, filled with the perpetual carefree days of a long summer childhood. In fact, eeking out a living as farmers where the soil was poor and stony was a hard, challenging existence for the family. The Transkei had been designated as a

ABOVE: Nelson's family struggled to farm the poor soil in the Transkei, the most fertile land being reserved for white farmers.
RIGHT: Collecting fresh water was one of the many tasks left to the women and girls of the village.

'bantustan' or black African homeland under the apartheid system – a place where black people were allowed to own and farm their own land. It was an area of scenic beauty, but it was not prime farming land. The finest agricultural land was retained by the whites.

Yet Mandela's family were not the most impoverished in the area. They were tribal aristocrats, albeit that they had fallen on hard times. Rolihlahla's father was Gadla Henry

Mphakanyiswa Mandela of the Thembu tribe, grandson of the Thembu King Ngubengcuka. Henry was the chief of Mvezo village (where Rolihlahla was born) on the banks of the Mbashe River until he resolutely defied a local white magistrate by refusing to respond to a summons in a dispute over livestock. The magistrate punished Henry by removing him as chief, whereupon Henry had to give up his home, his land and his cattle, moving his entire family from Mvezo to Qunu.

Although deprived of his position as a local chief, Henry retained his status within the Madiba clan, the ruling family of the Thembu tribe. He was an adviser to the Thembu King

Dalindyebo and also to Dalindyebo's son, Jongintaba, who became regent until Sabata (a younger son of Dalindyebo from a wife who perpetuated the royal birth line) was old enough to take the throne. The white overlords may have been able to depose Henry from his position as chief, but they could not erase his roots in the Thembu royal family, or destroy the respect that was afforded him by the local populace.

Despite his standing within the community, and his reputation as a great storyteller who held audiences spellbound as he related tales from the long history of the Xhosa nation (the Thembu had been part of the Xhosa nation

since the sixteenth century), Henry could neither read nor write. Rolihlahla, then aged seven, was to be the first of Henry's children to attend school. On a small hill just outside the village was a one-roomed, whitewashed schoolhouse with a mud floor and a tin roof that made raindrops sound like machinegun fire. It was traditional for children to be given an English name when they first started school and Rolihlahla's teacher, Miss Mdingane, gave him the name Nelson.

Two years later, Nelson's peaceful existence was to change immeasurably. His father, who divided his time between his wives and

LEFT: Young Xhosa women wearing traditional clothes and jewellery.
BELOW: A Xhosa village nestling on the hillside.

generally lived in Rolihlahla's mother's hut for one week in four, arrived early and was clearly unwell. Within a few days, he was dead. Having been identified as a bright, promising student, Nelson was 'adopted' by Jongintaba. Nosekeni Fanny took her son on a long trek, walking from sunrise to sunset, until they reached Mqhekezweni – The Great Place – royal palace of Chief Jongintaba. There were two large rectangular buildings and seven mud-brick roundhouses of a size that Nelson had never before seen. All were beautifully whitewashed and surrounded by gardens, fields of maize and orchards with a herd of cattle and hundreds of sheep grazing on the hillside. To the eyes of anyone from a city in Europe, America, or anywhere else in

the developed world in 1927, The Great Place would have looked like nothing more than a basic, rural, African farming community. To nine-year-old Nelson, it looked like paradise.

After a couple of days, Nosekeni Fanny said goodbye to her son, leaving him in the care of Jongintaba's family. He was given clothes to wear – the men in The Great Place wore Western-style suits and the women dresses – and Jongintaba's wife, No-England, treated Nelson just as though he were one of her own children. Their son, Justice, immediately became Nelson's hero. Four years older, tall and athletic, Justice appeared to Nelson to be 'everything a young man should be and everything I longed to be'.

Nelson attended the small school at The Great Place where he was taught English, Xhosa history and geography. There was plenty of time for him to explore his new home, but there were also chores to be done and Nelson continued to tend livestock. He became firm friends with Justice, although the older boy was not around all the time, having already been enrolled as a boarder at Clarkebury Boarding Institute sixty miles away.

At The Great Place, Nelson was to witness tribal gatherings when men came from far and wide to seek Jongintaba's help in settling disputes or to participate in the debates that were held concerning the implementation of new laws or steps that needed to be taken

RIGHT: Xhosa children outside a 'rondavel' hut in Nelson's home village of Qunu.

ABOVE: Nelson and his cousin, Justice, underwent the same initiation ceremony as these two young Xhosa men.

to deal with drought or disease. Everyone who came had the right to speak at these gatherings before Jongintaba guided them towards an agreed solution to whatever problem was under discussion. It was a truly democratic system in most respects, save for the fact that women were not allowed to participate. Jongintaba's wisdom, and having the chance to witness government in action, were to have a profound effect on Nelson.

When he was sixteen, Nelson was sent to Clarkebury, travelling there in Jongintaba's car and wearing his first-ever pair of shoes. At the school he was introduced to the Reverend Harris, who ran Clarkebury. Nelson had seen many white men since he went to live at The Great Place, but as Reverend Harris extended his hand to the young man whom he had just been told was being groomed and educated to become an adviser to the next Thembu King, Nelson realised that he had

never before shaken hands with a white man. In fact, he was to become very close to the Harris family. All students were expected to do chores after school and Nelson was assigned to help tend the Harrises' vegetable garden. The Reverend ran the school, which was also a teacher training college, in a strictly disciplined way, demanding respect from the teachers as well as the pupils and rarely letting slip his stern demeanour. Nelson, however, often saw him in moments of quiet contemplation in the garden and, as he grew to become a friend of the family, he saw the more mellow, relaxed side of Reverend Harris. He described how he came to understand that the Reverend had 'a public face and a private manner that were quite different from one another'. This was an important lesson for the young student, learning that someone like the Reverend had to behave differently when at work than he did when off duty. Neither attitude was an act, simply a different facet of the same character. In later life he would have to learn to do the same.

In the hallowed surroundings of Clarkebury, where the colonial buildings housed classrooms, libraries and dormitories, with individual Western-style houses also scattered around the campus, Nelson was given a glimpse of a different way of life. He also heard stories from the more well-travelled students about the exciting, almost mythical city of Johannesburg. To Nelson, it scarcely seemed possible that such a place could exist so close at hand – a city with miles of paved streets, boulevards of shops, hotels and theatres, buildings that soared up to eleven storeys high.

Such a place, however, was not where he saw his future. He remained set on a path that would lead him to the right hand of the Thembu King. Nelson had by now acquired another name, Dalibhunga, meaning 'creator of the council', given to him at his tribal initiation ceremony when he was circumcised

along with Justice and two dozen other boys. The ceremony, which lasted several days, required the initiates to be painted first with white ochre and later with red and to live together during this time, all contact with their families forbidden. Nelson struggled at first at Clarkebury in making the leap from his largely traditional tribal upbringing to the more 'Western' style of education he received there, but he was quick to adapt and achieved his 'Junior Certificate', which he required to progress to further education, in two years rather than the more usual three.

Nelson's father, Henry, had never been attracted to Christianity, reserving his faith for the traditional Xhosa religion, most notably Qamata, who, in Xhosa folklore, was the son of Thixo (the god of the sun), and

Jobela (the goddess of the earth). Qamata was said to have created the land, battling against a powerful sea serpent to do so, with the aid of four giants created by his mother. When he finally triumphed, the giants all lay down on the land to sleep and were turned to stone so that they could protect the land forever more. One of the giants became Table Mountain. Henry Mandela, like others who followed Qamata, would add a stone to any cairns, or mounds of stones, he came across on his travels in the hope that Qamata would then grant him good fortune. He was also an unofficial priest and officiated at various

RIGHT: Nelson around the time he attended Healdtown College in 1937.
BELOW: Nelson unveils a plaque at the opening of the museum, ten years after his release from prison.

religious ceremonies. But Henry held no prejudice against Christians. In fact, he befriended two Christian brothers from a tribe not normally on friendly terms with the Thembu and was not troubled by the fact that Nosekeni Fanny became a Christian after long discussions with them.

It was through the encouragement of these two brothers, who were Methodists, that Nelson first went to school and, when he went to live with Jongintaba's family, who were also Methodists, he continued to be brought up in the Christian faith. Clarkebury was built on Thembu land and was originally founded by Wesleyan missionaries. Wesleyans were Protestant Christians who followed the theology of the English brothers John and Charles Wesley, a movement that is now more commonly known as Methodism. In 1937, when Nelson progressed to Healdtown College just outside Fort Beaufort in the hills of the Eastern Cape, he remained within the Methodist fold as Healdtown was also a Wesleyan institution.

If Clarkebury had impressed Nelson, Healdtown quite took his breath away. The largest school in southern Africa, Healdtown boasted over one thousand students, both male and female. Due to the segregation laws, of course, all of the students were black, despite the fact that Fort Beaufort was a white town. The ivy-clad buildings stood proudly amid courtyards that lay in the shade of many trees, with a lush green valley stretching into the distance below and the surrounding hills providing a tranquil setting for serious study.

Established in 1845, the school would be forced to close during the unrest that swept South Africa in 1976, when its buildings were set alight. Re-opened as the smaller Healdtown Comprehensive School in 1994, it is the subject of ongoing renovation and restoration work.

Again like Clarkebury, Healdtown was run almost like a military establishment, not least because the principal was Dr Arthur Wellington, who claimed the Iron Duke as one of his ancestors. Nelson lived in a dormitory that housed forty young men and began each day when the first bell rang at 6.00am. Classes began at 8.00am and, with a break for lunch, lasted until 5.00pm.

Nelson studied hard, and made new

friends, some of whom were not of the Xhosa nation. Although Healdtown was predominantly a Xhosa institution, there were students from all over the country and beyond, even as far as Bechuanaland (now Botswana). While there was a natural tendency for students to congregate after classes mainly within their own tribal groups, this was Nelson's first real opportunity to socialize with non-Xhosas. He became a prefect, took up distance running and boxing and immersed himself in school life. He retained the reputation he had acquired at Clarkebury for having a keen intellect and unfailing memory, but described himself as 'simply a diligent worker'. His diligence led, after two years, to his progressing from Healdtown to Fort Hare University to study for a Bachelor of Arts degree.

While Nelson's father had told him many stories about the heroes and history of the Thembu and the Xhosa nation (and Nosekeni had shown herself to be equally gifted as a storyteller, sending her son off to sleep each night with wondrous tales of Thembu myth and legend), at Healdtown Nelson had started to learn more about the harsh realities of life for the black population of his homeland. As he matured, so his understanding of the world began to change. He was still enormously conservative in his outlook, pursuing his education with the sole aim of returning to fulfil his destiny within the Thembu clan, but he had now seen something of the wider world and was acquiring an appreciation of the injustices perpetrated by the white men

who dominated South Africa. Fort Hare was to witness the political awakening of Nelson Mandela when he began his crusade against such injustice.

From the time it was founded in 1916, Fort Hare quickly became the most important higher-education establishment for black Africans from territories all across sub-Saharan Africa and today has around 11,000 students on three separate campuses. The Fort Hare that Nelson Mandela attended, however, was somewhat different. On the original campus at Alice in the Eastern Cape, there were barely a few hundred students, but many of them would go on to become hugely influential figures in African politics. Chris Hani (leader of the South African Communist Party), Frank Mdlalose (first Premier of KwaZulu-Natal), Desmond Tutu (Archbishop of Cape Town and peace campaigner), Kenneth Kaunda (first President of Zambia), Robert Mugabe (President of Zimbabwe) and Oliver Tambo (ANC leader), among many others, all studied at Fort Hare.

When he enrolled at Fort Hare, Nelson knew several older students who had also attended Clarkebury and Healdtown, but not all of them acted as though they were pleased to see him. The older students tended to look down on the new arrivals and even held sway over them in such matters as their dormitory House Committees, where senior students ran the show, allocating chores to the juniors even though the seniors no longer shared the same dormitories. Nelson and a small group of newcomers took exception to

ABOVE: The Nelson Mandela Museum stretches over several locations around Mvezo and Qunu.

this and organized elections to vote in a new House Committee. Nelson was one of those elected by the student body and the juniors democratically seized power from the seniors. The ensuing furore ultimately involved the warden of the college, who decided that the juniors had shown themselves to be perfectly capable of running their own affairs and left them to it. Future clashes with the university establishment, however, were not to turn out quite so well for Nelson.

With his predisposition towards diligent hard work, Nelson progressed well with his studies, taking a particular interest in learning about the law, but also found time to join the football team, to improve his standing as a cross-country runner, to try his hand as an actor with the drama society and to join the Students' Christian Association. On Sundays, Nelson would visit neighbouring villages to teach Bible classes and one of the students also involved with the Christian Association was a young man called Oliver Tambo. Although he was not one of Nelson's closest associates at university, the two would later become inextricably linked through the ANC.

In his second term at Fort Hare, Nelson and his friends followed the progress of the war in Europe, as they had done since they arrived at the university in 1939, and Nelson was also elected to the Students Representative

Council. In a dispute over the poor food that was being given to the students and the lack of power afforded to the Council, Nelson and the other Council members resigned. While the others ultimately accepted reinstatement, Nelson stuck to his guns and was told that, once he had sat his exams at the end of term, he would be expelled unless he agreed to re-join the Council the following term. He returned to Mqhekezweni with a heavy heart, having passed his exams but knowing what Jongintaba would have to say.

As expected, Jongintaba told Nelson to sort things out with the university and return to finish his degree, no matter what principles he had to sacrifice or how much humble pie he would have to eat. Justice, who had been living in Cape Town but was also back at Mqhekezweni, was far more sympathetic towards his younger 'brother'. Then came a bombshell that left them both reeling. Jongintaba was starting to plan ahead, worrying about his old age, and was anxious to see his two sons settle down – so he had arranged marriages for both of them. Both young men were aghast, not least because the girl that Jongintaba had chosen for Nelson had long been in love with Justice. This was a situation that could have only one resolution. Justice and Nelson talked it over, agreed exactly what to do, plucked up their courage . . . and ran away.

RIGHT: Visitors at the entrance to one of the museum sites.

CHAPTER TWO

Surviving in Johannesburg

To finance their great escape, Nelson and Justice sold a couple of Jongintaba's cattle, the trader to whom they sold the beasts assuming that they were doing so with their father's permission. They then hired a car and driver to take them to a railway station where they could catch a train to Johannesburg.

Jongintaba, however, was one step ahead of them. The ticketmaster at the station recognized Nelson and Justice straight away, Jongintaba having already visited the station several days before, describing them both to the ticketmaster and warning him that they were runaways. The two ran back to the car and paid the driver to take them to the next station down the line, where they eventually managed to board a train that took them as far as Queenstown, although neither Nelson nor Justice found the train ride through the countryside in the least bit relaxing. For a black man to travel anywhere in South Africa at that time he had to have the correct identity papers and travel permits, documents showing that he had permission to travel and that stated the reason for his journey. These had to be signed by his employer or the local magistrate and correctly dated. Although Nelson and Justice had their identity passes, they had none of

PREVIOUS SPREAD AND LEFT: Nelson was amazed by the tall buildings and the number of motor cars when he first arrived in Johannesburg.

'There is no passion to be found in playing small – in settling for a life that is less than the one you are capable of living.'

NELSON MANDELA

the other documentation and, should any white police officer or railway official demand to see them, they faced being fined or even thrown in prison.

At Queenstown they planned to visit a relative who they hoped would be able to help them on the next stage of their journey. When they reached the relative's house, they were surprised to find Justice's uncle, Chief Mpondombini, paying a visit. They told him that they were on an errand for Jongintaba but that they had left home without the necessary documents, at which the chief immediately escorted them to the local magistrate, vouched for them as his nephews, and persuaded him to furnish them with all the travel documentation they required. But when the magistrate decided to make a quick phone call to his counterpart in the runaways' home district, their deception came unstuck. Jongintaba just happened to be sitting in the office talking to the magistrate in question when the call came through.

Furious, he demanded that the pair be arrested immediately. There was huge embarrassment in the Queenstown office and Nelson quickly stepped in to calm the situation. Through his legal studies at Fort Hare he knew that, aside from the small matter of the travel permits, they had not broken any serious laws. He persuaded the magistrate that, although they had lied to him, he had no real grounds to arrest them and that it would

ABOVE: Miners working a gold seam at Crown Mines in the 1930s, one-and-a-half miles underground.

not look good if he did so simply at the behest of their father. The magistrate ordered them out of his office. Their uncle was mortified at the deceit they had perpetrated and Nelson, his Christian upbringing having instilled in him a distinct appreciation of right and wrong, was ashamed at the lies they had told. The situation they were in, however, seemed to call for yet more of the same behaviour.

Justice then contacted a friend in Queenstown who knew someone who was planning to drive to Johannesburg. The driver took them along as passengers, but charged them a fee that ate up almost all of the money that they had left. When they arrived in the great city of Johannesburg, Nelson was overawed by the hustle and bustle of this thriving metropolis. At the time,

ABOVE: Spoil from the mines piled high on the outskirts of Johannesburg.
RIGHT: Nelson's philosophy was to reject all forms of racism and sexism, and to accept all forms of religion, which led to a tense meeting with Louis Farrakhan, leader of the Nation of Islam in 1996.

Johannesburg had a population of around half a million – today it is eight times that size. The car they were in wove through the traffic, more vehicles than Nelson had ever seen, and arrived at a large house in the suburbs where Nelson and Justice were offered a place to sleep for the night – the bare floor of the servants' quarters.

The next day the intrepid pair set out to make their fortunes, their first port of call being the Crown Mines offices on the hillside just outside the town. Johannesburg grew

up at the base of the Witwatersrand (White Water Reef), a mountain ridge that stretches for 170 miles through the Gauteng province. Gold from the reef had been mined since the early nineteenth century, but it was the Witwatersrand Gold Rush in 1886 that saw the small settlement of Johannesburg rapidly expand to become a major mining town. The ore mined from the reef was not always of the highest quality but the availability of cheap labour – black Africans like the men Nelson knew in Qunu, who left their farms and families to work in the reef mines – made the Witwatersrand mines hugely profitable. It is thought that 40 per cent of all of the gold ever dug out of the ground has come from the reef mines.

Having heard so much about the mines,

Nelson and Justice arrived at Crown Mines, Johannesburg's the largest mining operation, expecting to find a palatial office block and were disappointed at the somewhat ramshackle assortment of industrial shacks and sheds. They asked to see a man named Piliso, who had the power to hire or fire and to whom Jongintaba had written many months before to arrange for Justice to be given a clerical job at the mine. Piliso was surprised that Justice had turned up without his father having warned of his arrival, and even more surprised that he had brought his brother in tow. Nevertheless, they were both given jobs, Justice as a clerk and Nelson as a mine policeman. He was required to check passes at the gate and patrol the living quarters where hundreds of miners lived in barracks

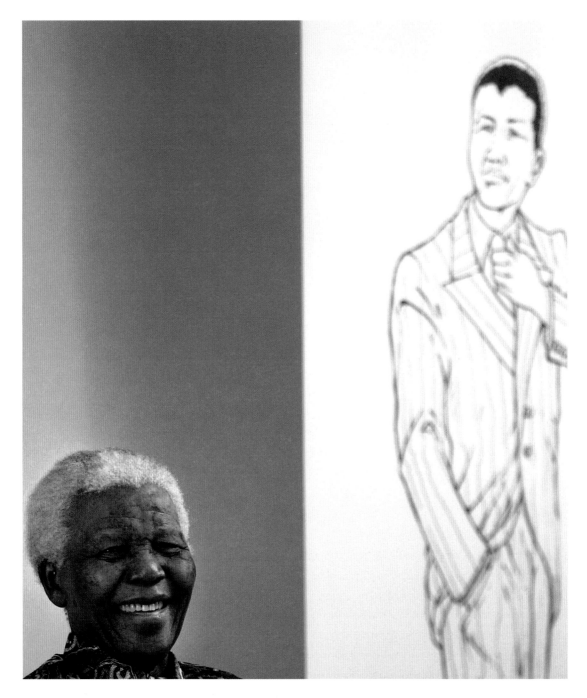

ABOVE: Nelson with an image from a comic book about his life, showing him as a young man in a sharp suit.

RIGHT: Nelson explained to fashion icon Pierre Cardin that he was comfortable in his patterned shirts, most of which were given to him as gifts.

huts, crammed in, sleeping elbow to elbow in concrete bunks.

It wasn't long before Piliso found out that the two runaways were working without Jongintaba's permission and, predictably, he was incensed by their deception. He sacked them and told them to go home, but the pair made one more attempt to establish themselves at the mine, contacting one of Jongintaba's oldest friends, Dr Xuma, who was President of the African National Congress, an organization that was to have a profound effect on Nelson's future. Dr Xuma used his connections, without realizing that he was helping Justice and Nelson to con their way back into Crown Mines employment, to go over the head of Piliso and recommend the pair to one of Piliso's bosses. When Justice and Nelson turned up at the mine again, it wasn't long before they ran into Piliso, who promptly threw them out again. They decided that Justice would head into town to find them somewhere to stay while Nelson got their belongings together and followed on. It was while he was heading towards the mine gate that a friend of Nelson's offered to help carry the suitcase. When the case was searched, as a matter of routine, by the gate guard, he found, wrapped up in some of Nelson's clothes, a loaded revolver.

Nelson's friend was immediately surrounded by guards, arrested and hustled off to the police station. Nelson followed on. The revolver had been his father's and, as he explained to the police at his earliest opportunity, he had brought it to the big city in case he needed it for protection. Nelson's friend was released and Nelson made his first court appearance,

BELOW: Nelson's portrait in a shirt and tie, carried at a rally in London in 1990, contrasts with . . .
RIGHT: Nelson in another patterned shirt, with an HIV/AIDS awareness ribbon symbol instead of a tie.

ABOVE: Oliver Tambo worked tirelessly for the ANC and to secure Nelson's freedom.

ABOVE: Nelson, whose first home as an adult was in Soweto, celebrates with the Soweto Gospel Choir after they won their second Grammy Award in 2008.

whereupon he was fined for being found in possession of the loaded weapon. He counted himself lucky to have been let off so lightly.

Having decided that he wanted to study law, Nelson persuaded one of his cousins in Johannesburg to introduce him to an estate agent named Walter Sisulu. Sisulu was six years older than Nelson, and his business revolved around finding properties or smallholdings for Africans, in the areas where black Africans were permitted to own property, and he was fast becoming a highly respected figure among black Africans. Little did they know it at the time, but they were to become lifelong friends. Sisulu was delighted to hear that Nelson wanted to become a lawyer and introduced him to a Jewish lawyer named Lazar Sidelsky.

Sidelsky had been born in Johannesburg, the son of immigrant Jewish refugees from Lithunia. The family bought a farm in the Transvaal but, just as Sidelsky was about to begin studying law at the University of Witwatersrand, his father died. Sidelsky paid his way through university by playing in a jazz band. When he qualified as a lawyer, his firm, Witkin, Sidelsky and Eidelman, championed the employment and education of black people. He gave Nelson every encouragement to resume his university education and take up law, taking him on as an articled clerk. Nelson regarded him as the first white man to have shown him any real respect and their

LEFT: Nelson shares a platform with his old friend, South African Communist Party leader Joe Slovo, in Cape Town, 1990.

friendship was to flourish during the course of the next sixty years.

While Nelson made friends easily, he retained the capacity to disappoint and disillusion those who extended the hand of friendship to him. When he arranged, through his cousin, to lodge with the Reverend Mabutho, an Anglican minister and fellow Thembu well known to his family, Nelson neglected to tell Mabutho that he was in Johannesburg very much against his father's wishes. The reverend asked him to leave but also helped him to find other accommodation with a neighbour. Nelson rented a shack with a tin roof at the back of the neighbour's house. He had no electricity or running water, but he was happy to be in his own place.

From his salary of £2 per week, Nelson had to pay his rent, feed himself, pay his bus fares to work (which meant that, more often than not, he walked the six miles there and back) and keep some money back to buy candles so that he could study at night. He also had to pay fees to the University of South Africa in order to complete his BA by correspondence course before he could begin studying for a law degree. In 1942, Nelson completed his BA and moved to live closer to the centre of Johannesburg at the WNLA – Witwatersrand Native Labour Association. The organization recruited mine workers and it was here that Jongintaba stayed on his occasional visits to Johannesburg. It was here, too, that Nelson met his adoptive father for the last time. They were able to set aside their differences and Jongintaba seemed

ABOVE: Nelson's university, Witwatersrand, always a hotbed of radicalism, is bombarded with police teargas rounds in 1987.

pleased and proud that Nelson was devoting himself to becoming a lawyer.

A few months later, Jongintaba died. The news reached Nelson and Justice too late for them to make it back to Mqhekezweni for the funeral, but they returned nonetheless. Justice now had important responsibilities to assume as the new chief. His life was now to revolve around the administration of tribal affairs, just as his father's had done, but Nelson could no longer contemplate settling into a minor role as a provincial civil servant. In Johannesburg he had begun to learn more than simply how to become a lawyer. He had seen the true scale of the social injustice that blighted his country. He had witnessed how white people lived in luxury while black people were condemned to endure grinding poverty in order to support the lifestyles of the whites. The simple country boy had outgrown his limited ambitions, developing a political awareness that was leading to political activism.

At Witkin, Sidelsky and Eidelman, Nelson had become friends with another clerk named Gaur Radebe, who was a member of both the ANC and the South African Communist Party (SACP). Nat Bregman, a white clerk who had started at the firm shortly before Nelson's arrival, was also a member of the Communist Party. Nelson enjoyed long, philosophical debates with his work colleagues (although Sidelsky repeatedly warned him that if he got involved in politics, he would end up in jail) and Nat took him along to some Communist Party meetings but, perhaps because his own

family were of noble birth, with their roots in the ruling clan of the Thembu stretching back to the point where the haze of history mingles with the mist of folklore, he saw his country's problems in a different light. 'I was just becoming aware of the history of racial oppression in my own country and saw the struggle in South Africa as purely racial,' he later wrote. His communist friends, on the other hand, 'saw South Africa's problems through the lens of the class struggle'.

Nelson enrolled at the University of Witwatersrand in 1942 to study law. 'Wits', as it is still commonly known today, owed its existence, as does Johannesburg, to the mining industry, having grown out of the South African School of Mines. The mining school had been founded in 1896 in Kimberley, but moved to Johannesburg in 1904 developing through several name changes until finally becoming the University of Witwatersrand in 1922. By the time Nelson began studying law there, Wits boasted almost 3,000 students – male and female, black and white. The university's first principal, Professor Jan Hofmeyr, had decreed that Wits 'should know no distinctions of class, wealth, race or creed', but racist attitudes were so endemic in South Africa's white population that black students were often left in no doubt about the opinions of some of the students and staff. When he sat down in a lecture hall, Nelson regularly experienced the humiliation of having white students move to sit further away from him.

Yet not all of the white students had such an abhorrent attitude. Like every university campus, Wits had its fair share of political idealists and young firebrands, not least because it was known as an institution that pursued a policy of non-discrimination. It would continue to stand against this injustice throughout the apartheid era. Among the many student activists Nelson met at Wits was Joe Slovo. Like Lazar Sidelsky, Slovo was the son of Jewish refugees from Lithuania. He was so inspired by the stories of the communist Soviet forces battling against the fascist Germans in Eastern Europe that he left Wits to volunteer for military service. He finished his law degree when he returned from the war.

There were many committed communists like Slovo (he was to become General Secretary of the SACP) who railed against racism in South Africa and were to become integral to the ANC cause. Nelson continued to attend meetings and participate in discussions about South Africa's future, eventually joining the ANC in 1943. Many of the ANC meetings took place at Walter Sisulu's house. The estate agent's home always seemed to be filled with political campaigners, some of whom, including Nelson, ended up living there from time to time when they were otherwise homeless. Although not one of the political activists, Evelyn Mase was also a regular visitor to the house. Training as a nurse with Walter's wife, Albertina (Nelson had been best man at the Sisulus' wedding), Evelyn was Walter's cousin and Nelson swiftly fell in love with this 'quiet, pretty girl from the countryside', despite – perhaps even

ABOVE: Oliver Tambo showing the Mpondo tribe 'rites of passage' scarring on his face.

because of – the fact that she took no interest in politics. As a Jehovah's Witness she was forbidden to participate in politics.

Before long, Nelson proposed to Evelyn and they were married in 1944 in a civil ceremony at the Native Commissioner's

Court in Johannesburg. They could not afford a big wedding and the ceremony involved little more than appending their signatures to the required legal documents. The couple were to have four children: two sons, Madiba Thembekile (born in 1946) and Makgatho (born in 1950); and two daughters, Makaziwe (who was born in 1947 but died at the age of just nine months) and Makaziwe (born in 1953 and named in honour of her sister).

After a period living with relatives,

LEFT: Makaziwe Mandela receiving a peace award on behalf of her father in Boston, USA, in 1986.
BELOW: Nelson meets Oliver Tambo for the first time in 28 years in Stockholm, Sweden, 1990.

the Mandelas were eventually allocated a home in a municipal housing project called Orlando West, part of an area known as the South Western Townships, which would later acquire the acronym Soweto. Nelson completed his three-year term as an articled clerk with Witkin, Sidelsky and Eildelman in 1947 and began studying full-time for his law degree with the help of a loan from the South African Institute of Race Relations. While he loved to spend time with Thembekile, nicknamed 'Thembi', bathing his son and telling, telling and re-telling bedtime stories just like any other proud father, Nelson's political involvement often caused great

ABOVE: Sophiatown, Johannesburg, 1954.

upheaval in his domestic life. His house became rather like Walter Sisulu's home, regularly filled with visitors and family guests who lodged there whenever necessary. It was an accepted custom that such hospitality would always be extended to family members. Nelson, however, was not always around to act as a hospitable host.

Having become a member of the ANC in 1943, Nelson was part of a delegation that went to visit ANC president Dr Xuma at what Nelson described as 'his rather grand home in Sophiatown'. This was a suburb of Johannesburg that had become well known as a cultural centre for black musicians, writers and artists. Dr Xuma had a surgery at his house there as well as a small farm. The delegation recognized the enormous contribution that Xuma had made to the ANC over the years, but his 'old guard' policy of registering official complaints, sending letters and lobbying politicians was doing little to further the cause of black Africans. The delegation, which advocated the establishment of an ANC Youth League to recruit new members and gather support for more concerted, higher-profile protests, did not receive the president's blessing. Ironically, Sophiatown was even then registering on the radar of the municipal authorities. As the white suburbs around it expanded, Sophiatown, inhabited by over 50,000 black Africans and more than 5,000 mixed-race, Indian or Chinese, became an annoyance to its white neighbours and plans were laid to destroy it. In February 1955, 2,000 policemen stormed into the area

and forcibly removed the local residents, relocating them to Soweto and other suitably designated areas. Nelson Mandela was among those leading the resistance against the police action. Sophiatown was bulldozed and later rebuilt as the Whites-only Triomf (or Triumph), although it was redesignated as Sophiatown after the fall of the apartheid regime. Dr Xuma's house was one of only two to survive the bulldozers and is now a heritage centre.

The ANC delegation established the Youth League under the leadership of Anton Lembede, with Walter Sisulu, Oliver Tambo and Nelson Mandela also among the sixty-strong group. They were soon to embark on more direct protests against the South African regime, intent on transforming the ANC into a radical movement that would involve the masses in bringing about self-determination and majority rule for the people of South Africa.

Nelson fully realized that theirs would be a long struggle requiring huge sacrifice. He looked to Mahatma Gandhi's example of civil disobedience and peaceful protest, Ghandi having employed such tactics as a lawyer in South Africa before the First World War when fighting for the resident Indian communities' civil rights, but he feared that far more drastic action would ultimately be required.

RIGHT: Downtown Johannesburg around the same period.

CHAPTER THREE

Into Battle

The ANC had been instrumental in working with other South African trade unions to set up the African Mine Workers' Union in 1941. There were upwards of 400,000 miners in South Africa working mainly in the coal, diamond and gold industries, and the wealth buried deep in the country's soil continues to be exploited today as the country remains a major producer of chrome, manganese, platinum and vanadium, among other valuable metals and minerals.

The black Africans who dug such riches out of the ground were paid the paltry sum of two shillings a day. Their white counterparts earned twelve times more. As Nelson well knew, having worked as a guard at the mines, the men came from all over the country, they spoke many languages, they were housed in strict security and they were spied upon by the mine owners. This made it all the more difficult for them to be organized under one umbrella, and all the more impressive that it had been achieved in the form of the AMWU. What truly impressed Nelson, however, was that these men were willing to put aside long-standing rivalries and stand together to fight for a higher wage. In 1946 the AMWU demanded an increase to ten shillings a day for its members, along with improvements in their living and working conditions. Their demands were ignored and the men voted to strike, full in the knowledge that it was illegal for a black worker to go out on strike. They stood to lose not only their jobs and their livelihoods, but in many cases their homes and their liberty. Some were to lose their lives.

The strike in August 1946 lasted for a week. Police attacked pickets outside the mines with heavy truncheons and bayonets and fired live rounds at the protestors. During one peaceful march, the police attacked the procession, killing several workers. Nelson had a number of relatives working in the mines and visited them to show his support. The AMWU's dedication to the strike could not be faulted but it cost them dear – over 1,200 workers were wounded and a dozen were killed. It was clear to Nelson that his countrymen were willing to make sacrifices to fight for higher wages, and clear that the different ethnic groups could be organized into a single militant body (something that the old guard of the ANC had always said was impossible), but would they agree to the same in the struggle for their civil liberties?

An example was set when the Indian community in South Africa united in protest

> **'I learned that courage was not the absence of fear, but the triumph over it. The brave man is not he who does not feel afraid, but he who conquers that fear.'**
>
> NELSON MANDELA

PREVIOUS SPREAD: Police keep supporters away from the court house in Pretoria as the verdict is announced in the Rivonia Trial.
LEFT: To help curb violence in the 1990s, Nelson pressed for the carrying of traditional weapons to be banned.

against new laws passed in 1946 that restricted their movements, banning them from owning property or living in certain neighbourhoods or from running their businesses in all but specifically designated areas. The Natal Indian Congress, which Mahatma Gandhi had helped to establish in 1894, in conjunction with the Transvaal Indian Congress, began a two-year programme of peaceful mass protests, staging rallies in areas from which they were prohibited and suffering violent suppression at the hands of the police. Over 2,000 were jailed. Although they did not participate directly in the Indian protests, other groups, including the ANC and its Youth League, expressed their support for the Indians and Nelson greatly admired the way that the Indians had organized 'an extraordinary

protest against colour suppression in a way that Africans and the ANC had not'.

Nelson's commitment to the ANC and the same sort of 'diligent', methodical work that had carried him through his school days saw him progress to the executive committee of the Transvaal ANC in 1947 and to become national secretary of the Youth League in 1948. Throughout this time he was growing in confidence not only in his own belief that Africans needed to work to take control of their own destiny, but also in his skills as an organizer and as an orator. No longer content simply to listen and learn, he had developed his

AL GROUP T.I.CONGR

ABOVE: Nelson admired the non-violent protests of Mahatma Gandhi and his son, Manilal, seen here campaigning in Johannesburg in 1939.

ABOVE: Daniel Malan, the father of apartheid, with his wife outside No 10 Downing Street in London.

own opinions about the future of his people. He was wary when the Indian Congresses joined forces with the ANC in 1947. The African People's Organization, an association of Coloureds (in South Africa there were four official classifications of people: Whites, Blacks, Indians and Coloureds – Coloured people were of mixed ancestry) later also allied themselves with the ANC, as did the SACP. Nelson's concern was that these other organizations would dominate the ANC due to their members' extensive political experience and superior education. He was also worried that their close involvement would distract the ANC from what he saw as its primary role – fighting for rights of black Africans. The others, after all, had different axes to grind, different issues to address.

All of the organizations were, however, united against a common enemy which, in 1948, took on an even more sinister form. In the South African elections that year, the National Party swept to power with its leader, Daniel François Malan, warning of the dire threat the increasingly dissatisfied Blacks posed to white rule. Malan was a highly educated man with degrees in mathematics and science as well as being a former minister in the Dutch Reformed Church. He was, however, determined to protect and maintain white supremacy in South Africa,

LEFT: Regina Elizabeth Brooks and Zulu Richard Kumalo, a police sergeant, pictured with their baby outside Johannesburg Magistrates Court in 1954, where they were convicted of living together illegally.

seeing the growing discontent among the black population as a dangerous problem and expressing the solution to that problem in a manifesto for apartheid. The national party's scaremongering won them thousands of votes from worried, affluent Whites. Blacks, of course, could not vote and Indians and Coloureds had only limited voting rights. Apartheid meant, quite literally, 'apartness' and was a term coined to describe the way that racial discrimination and segregation in South Africa was to become official government policy – backed up by the full force of the law.

The National Party swiftly moved to enact laws that would formalize and enforce the hitherto patchy approach to racial discrimination. The Prohibition of Mixed Marriages Act of 1949 made inter-racial marriages illegal; the Immorality Act of 1950 made it illegal to have sexual relations with anyone of a different race; the Suppression of Communism Act of 1950 banned the South African Communist Party and any other political party the government perceived as having communist sympathies; the Group Areas Act of 1950 prohibited people of different race from living in the same neighbourhoods and forced relocations were soon to come; the Reservation of Separate Amenities Act of 1953 meant that public places and services, from beaches, restaurants and parks to buses, hospitals and schools, were to be segregated, with the best amenities reserved and signposted for 'Whites Only'. More laws, more regulations and even greater

suppression of non-Whites was to follow.

The ANC's response was to adopt a policy of peaceful non-cooperation and civil disobedience. At their December 1949 conference in Bloemfontein the congress ratified the proposals drawn up by Nelson and the Youth League for a Programme of Action that would involve boycotts, strikes, demonstrations and other forms of passive mass action. Youth League members, having campaigned long and hard among the rank and file of the ANC, had enough support to depose the conservative Dr Xuma as the ANC's leader, installing Dr James Sebe Moroka as president. Dr Moroka, the great-grandson of a Tswana chief, was a medical doctor who had graduated from Edinburgh University. He was a well-known figure in South African politics but was also keen to adopt the Youth League's militant tactics, the sort of strategy eschewed by Dr Xuma. Also at the Bloemfontein conference, Walter Sisulu was elected secretary-general of the ANC while Oliver Tambo became a member of the national executive. The Youth League was in the ascendant, but Nelson could only watch from far-distant Johannesburg as the law firm for which he then worked would not give him two days off to attend the conference.

Nelson immediately became involved in planning an ANC National Day of Protest, but was upstaged by the SACP, which quickly gathered support for a strike on 1 May 1950.

LEFT: In the early 1950s, Nelson became President of the ANC Youth League.

The government's response was to ban all public gatherings on 1 May. Over two-thirds of African workers stayed at home that day and, in the evening, Nelson and Walter Sisulu joined a crowd in Orlando West that had gathered to celebrate Freedom Day despite the government ban. Shots rang out and the police appeared, charging into the crowd on horseback, hacking at the demonstrators with their batons. Nelson and Sisulu took cover indoors as chaos ensued outside. There were scores of injured among the crowd and at least eighteen Africans were killed by the police.

Nevertheless, the ANC resolved to proceed with its National Day of Protest, dedicating the protest to the eighteen who had died on 1 May. Nelson busied himself in the ANC's offices, coordinating the ANC activities in different regions throughout the country while others toured the provinces, drumming up support for the action that was planned for 26 June. On the day, the ANC's first attempt to organize a national event went every bit as well as they could have hoped. The majority of black workers in cities did not show up for work, black-owned businesses did not open their doors and thousands took to the streets to demonstrate. Nelson was ecstatic at their success, later writing that he 'felt the exhilaration that springs from the success of a well-planned battle against the enemy and the sense of comradeship that is born of fighting against formidable odds'.

Over the course of the following eighteen months, Nelson became president of the Youth League and was instrumental in drafting

a resolution calling for the government to repeal the unjust laws that they had instituted and abandon plans to introduce laws that would further infringe the human rights and civil liberties of South Africa's non-white population. They set a deadline of 29 February 1952 for the government to comply with their demands, otherwise the ANC would stage mass demonstrations on 6 April to launch a 'Campaign for the Defiance of Unjust Laws'. The April date was significant in that it was the day that white South Africans were preparing to celebrate the third centenary of the landing of Dutch pioneer Jan van

LEFT: Boxing training kept Nelson fit, although he never fought after taking up politics.
BELOW: Nelson's beard came and went many times over the years.

ABOVE: Nelson squares up to former World Heavyweight Boxing Champion Lennox Lewis in 2001.

Riebeeck at what was to become Cape Town. It marked the birth of the nation, or the dawn of slavery, depending on whether you were white or black.

On 6 April, the vast majority of black

ABOVE: Under Apartheid, Nelson and Princess Caroline of Monaco (seen here in 2007) could have been arrested for holding hands in public.
RIGHT: Nelson, Walter Sisulu and Harrison Motlana during a break in the Defiance Campaign trial in 1952.

Africans, including schoolchildren, boycotted the centenary celebrations. There were ANC rallies in Johannesburg, Pretoria, Port Elizabeth, Durban and Cape Town. Professor Zachariah Matthews, under whom Nelson had studied law at Fort Hare, addressed the gathering in Port Elizabeth, stressing that the fate of the African people lay in their own hands and that 'only the African people themselves will ever rid themselves of political subjugation, economic exploitation and social degradation.' Nelson, meanwhile, had been appointed national volunteer-in-chief for the forthcoming civil disobedience campaign and was talking to trade union members and other groups to recruit volunteers for mass protests. These were people who were to walk into proscribed areas without permits, use 'Whites Only' entrances at railway stations, use 'Whites Only' sections of the Post Office and otherwise disregard, in groups, the segregation regulations. Nelson stressed to them that, 'No matter what the authorities did, they could not retaliate . . . they must respond to violence with non-violence; discipline must be maintained at all costs.'

LEFT: Sports organisations began boycotting South Africa in the mid-1960s but by 1993 Manchester United was back on tour.
ABOVE: Nelson meets United star Ryan Giggs.

Nelson required his volunteers to sign a pledge that committed each one of them 'to serve my country and my people in accordance with the directives of the National Volunteer Corps and to participate fully and without reservations to the best of my ability in the Campaign for the Defiance of Unjust laws. I shall obey the orders of my leader under whom I shall be placed and strictly abide by the rules and regulations of the National Volunteer Corps framed from time to time. It shall be my duty to keep myself physically, mentally and morally fit.'

Following the initial action on 6 April, the campaign began in earnest on 26 June. Nelson was involved in one of the demonstrations on that day, delivering a letter to the local magistrate in Boksburg, to the east of Johannesburg, informing him that fifty volunteers intended to enter an area under his jurisdiction that day without the required permits. A crowd of press reporters and photographers covered the delivery of the note and still more were there when the volunteers were duly arrested later that day. Nelson and Oliver Tambo observed the demonstration from a distance, watching as the police, showing uncharacteristic restraint, apprehended the volunteers, who included Walter Sisulu. Nelson and Tambo then attended a meeting to discuss how the day's events had gone and were leaving that meeting when they, too, were arrested – for violating a curfew.

On that first day of the Defiance Campaign, 250 volunteers were arrested. Most were punished with a few days in prison or a fine of around £10. Some were released without charge. Nelson redoubled his efforts as an

BELOW: Nelson in the 'Mandela & Tambo' office in Johannesburg in 1952.
RIGHT: After being banned, Nelson came up with the 'M-Plan' to maintain lines of communication within the ANC.

ABOVE: Nelson organised protests against the destruction of Sophiatown.

organizer, coordinator and troubleshooter within the ANC and, in an attempt to crush the Defiance Campaign, the government decided to arrest key ANC personnel. At the end of July 1952, police officers arrived at the law firm where Nelson worked and arrested him. He was charged under the Suppression of Communism Act. He stood trial in September along with twenty other prominent ANC and Defiance Campaign leaders, their court appearances prompting thousands to march in the streets in peaceful protest. It was Nelson's proud boast that 'during the six months of the campaign, there was not a single act of violence on our part'. The judge at his trial agreed, stating in court that Nelson and the ANC had encouraged their supporters 'to avoid violence in any shape or form'. This was reflected in his sentence of nine months' hard labour – suspended for two years. During the course of the Defiance Campaign, 8,500 volunteers participated in events and the ANC membership increased fivefold to over 100,000. They drew international publicity and had proved that Africans were prepared to unite behind their cause. It was an immense achievement, but it was only the beginning.

More and more of Nelson's life was now revolving around his activities with the ANC, of which he became deputy president. He also became a 'banned' person, meaning that the government was restricting him to his home district of Johannesburg and that he could

LEFT: Walter Sisulu in 1989, following his release after 26 years in prison.

not travel, attend meetings or attend public gatherings for six months. The banning notices were intended to make it difficult for movements like the ANC to communicate with and organize their membership. There were, of course, no internet communications in those days, no mobile phones, no telephone landlines in most black households, so, for the ANC leadership, spreading a message often meant physically visiting the group they needed to contact. Nelson had learned to drive in 1952 and spent a great deal of time ferrying ANC colleagues from meeting to meeting or travelling to provincial centres to keep everyone informed of the latest plans and developments. Being banned made life difficult, so he came up with the Mandela Plan, or 'M-Plan'.

The M-Plan was instigated to allow the ANC to function and communicate, even if it became, like the SACP, an illegal organization prohibited from having any kind of public meetings. Information was to be passed on through 'hubs' with the centre of a hub at the lowest level being the member responsible for passing information to fellow members who lived in his street. He in turn would receive his information from an area hub, who would receive messages from a regional or provincial hub, and so on, right up to the national executive body. In effect, this is the way that military units are organized or, from the South African Government's point of view, the way that terrorists operate.

The M-Plan was never 100 per cent effective, but Nelson did find other ways to circumvent the banning orders that were employed against him. Having worked for a number of legal firms since leaving Witkin, Sidelsky and Eildelman, including a company where one of the partners was a former WWII pilot who was hugely supportive of the ANC cause and would later illegally fly senior members of the party to safety out of the country, Nelson set up his own law firm in August 1952. Working alone, with only a secretary to help him, he quickly had more clients than he could handle and, with the help of a loan from Lazar Sidelsky, Nelson soon went into partnership with Oliver Tambo.

In December 1952 the law firm of Mandela & Tambo moved into offices in central Johannesburg opposite the magistrates' court. Their building, owned by Indians, was one of the few in the centre of the city where black businesses could rent offices. They soon discovered, however, that, as black men, they were not allowed to have offices in the city without government permission. When they applied for the correct authorization, their application was turned down. Nelson saw this as an attempt by the authorities to shut down South Africa's first black law firm. There were numerous other black lawyers working in the country, but no other firms established and run by black Africans. Moving out of their offices to an area miles away where the authorities would allow them to do business would have made it almost impossible for many of their clients to reach them. They stayed put, working under the ever-present threat of eviction, dealing with some of Johannesburg's poorest people who were often confused and intimidated by the segregation laws.

Families who had lived and worked in an area for generations were suddenly told that they were breaking the law just by being in their own homes. There were people whose jobs meant that they ran the risk of breaking the 11.00pm curfew imposed on black Africans, or who had inadvertently walked through a 'Whites Only' door in a government building. Mandela & Tambo took on hundreds of cases, working for minimal fees, sometimes no fees at all, determined not to be forced out of central Johannesburg and thus abandon their people. As Nelson later put it: 'No attorney worth his salt would easily agree to do that.'

There was, however, another good reason for keeping the law practice going. Nelson handled many cases that required him to travel outside of Johannesburg for appearances in provincial courts. In order to do so, he would apply to have his bans lifted for a limited period. Permission was generally granted and it became a useful way to show people in other parts of the country that a black lawyer, an ANC leader, was working hard on their behalf in Johannesburg. Nelson's road trips helped to bolster support in areas where the M-plan had not been fully adopted.

In 1953, his bans having expired, Nelson became fully involved in organizing protests against the planned 'Western Area Removal' scheme, which would see not only Sophiatown but also neighbouring districts,

ABOVE: Another Nelson would have come in handy with the workload at 'Mandela & Tambo', but perhaps not in the shape of this 1991 waxwork model.

being cleared for redevelopment as white suburbs. The residents were to be rehoused elsewhere according to their official ethnic classification. The peaceful protests of the ANC demonstrated their growing strength and attracted international attention but Nelson knew that the 'removals' would go ahead in any case. In the meantime, many more protesters were arrested and suffered at the hands of the police. Nelson was slowly coming round to the idea that the ANC might have to move on from peaceful protests to more forceful action.

When Walter Sisulu told him that he had been invited to speak at an international peace conference in Bucharest, Nelson helped him to secure a false passport that would get him out of the country. Without the approval or knowledge of the ANC executive, Nelson also suggested that Walter extend his trip from Bucharest, in the then-communist Romania, to the Soviet Union and China.

ABOVE: Police disperse a crowd outside the Drill Hall where the 1956 Treason Trial was underway.

During those visits, Walter was to make discreet enquiries about acquiring weapons and military training for ANC personnel for a future armed struggle in South Africa.

In the meantime, protests and rallies continued and the pressure of his work and his political activities led to Nelson spending more and more time away from home, not least on the many occasions when he was arrested. One such incident, in September 1953, came when he was travelling to the Orange Free State to deal with a legal case he had taken on. His bans had been lifted but, when he walked into the courthouse in the small town of Villiers, he was immediately arrested and charged under the Suppression of Communism Act. Nelson was forced to resign from the ANC and was served with banning orders that precluded him from attending any meetings or leaving Johannesburg for the next two years. This lead to his watching, and advising, from the sidelines as the ANC continued its campaigns, but his workload – legal cases and keeping in touch with ANC activities – never really diminished. He would leave home early in the morning and, when his day in the office was over, he had ANC business to attend to, eventually returning home late at night. Evelyn and their children barely saw Nelson at all, although he often took Thembi with him to a gym in the local community centre where they trained with a group of boxers. Nelson did not step into the ring to fight properly once he had become involved in politics, but he found the physical training helped to relieve stress and tension.

The tension at home, however, continued to escalate. It was Evelyn's dearest wish that they would one day leave Johannesburg and return home to the Transkei, where Nelson could practise law and, as he had once thought was his destiny, act as an adviser to the Thembu Royal Family. Away from Johannesburg they could have a more normal family life. Nelson's family in Mqhekezweni were also keen for him to return but, for Nelson, that would mean giving up politics and the freedom struggle. Nelson tried to explain to Evelyn 'that politics was not a distraction, but my lifework, that it was an essential and fundamental part of my being'. Evelyn's religious beliefs, of course, set politics well below family commitments and the gulf that had opened between husband and wife relentlessly widened. By 1955, their differences were putting an unbearable strain on their marriage and when Nelson was arrested towards the end of the year and kept in prison for two weeks, he returned home to an empty house. Evelyn and the children had moved in with her brother. They were now officially separated.

By 1955 there were many organized political groups in South Africa speaking out against the government's apartheid policies. Many of these were inspired by the ANC successes, others had long been operating under their own agendas, but

LEFT: No more bans, no more prisons – Nelson in front of 120,000 people two days after his release in 1990.

when they massed at Kliptown, southwest of Johannesburg, for a joint Congress of the People rally over two days in June 1955, it gave the South African Government serious cause for concern. The 3,000 delegates from different organizations were harassed by police every step of the way and the rally was eventually broken up by the authorities, but not before the delegates had agreed on the wording of the Freedom Charter. This document called for racial equality in all walks of life in South Africa, land reforms, employment reforms, equal rights in education and the freedom for people to live where they chose. Essentially, it called for the dismantling of apartheid and a new beginning for South Africa.

Nelson, still with a banning order in force, watched the proceedings in secret from the periphery of the crowd, careful not to be seen. When the police finally moved in to end the gathering, methodically checking and noting the identity of everyone involved, he escaped disguised as a milkman. There was even greater subterfuge to follow as, shortly after his two-year ban was lifted, in March 1956 Nelson was served with a five-year banning order. This time, however, he decided not to comply so meekly with the ban. 'When I was first banned,' he admitted, 'I abided by the rules . . .' By now he had come to view things differently and believed that, 'To allow my activities to be circumscribed by my opponent was a form of defeat and I resolved not to become my own jailer.'

The state, of course, was more than willing to fulfil the role of jailer to Nelson Mandela. The Congress of the People sparked a determined clampdown by the government on what the authorities saw as subversive groups and, in December 1956, Nelson was arrested in a dawn raid on his home. Police ransacked the house and took Nelson away as his children, staying with him at the time, looked on in horror. He was charged with high treason, as were 155 others who were arrested at the same time or over the following few days across the country. The government had rounded up the entire leadership of the ANC in one fell swoop. They were locked up in Johannesburg Prison, known as The Fort, in appalling conditions but, with so many of them having struggled to meet in recent years because of banning orders, there was some jubilation at being confined together where they could talk freely at last. They spent two weeks in The Fort before attending a preliminary trial hearing that lasted for four days. The state based its case on the activities and demands of the ANC over the past four years and the wording of the Freedom Charter, all of which, it maintained, constituted a plot to overthrow the South African Government. High treason was punishable by death. After four days, bail was granted and Nelson, along with Oliver Tambo, who had also been arrested, began trying to deal with his backlog of legal cases while also preparing their defence for a trial that was to drag on for more than four years.

RIGHT: Treason Trialists, some giving the ANC 'thumbs up' salute, with Nelson near the middle of the third row from the bottom.

TREASON TRIAL

DECEM
195

the
JSED

CHAPTER FOUR

Prisoner 46664

The treason trial meant that Nelson spent most of his time working out ways to beat the charges laid against him. The law firm of Mandela & Tambo suffered tremendously as both men struggled to keep up with their workload. The situation became slightly less stressful when the first stage of the trial drew to a close in September 1957. The second stage, once the magistrate had determined that there was a valid case against the accused, was to take place in the Supreme Court. Before these proceedings began, however, a year after the initial arrests, the government dropped the charges against sixty-one of the accused, due to lack of evidence against them. These sixty-one included Oliver Tambo and Chief Albert Luthuli.

Chief Luthuli was a former teacher and college lecturer who had been involved in politics at a local level for many years before joining the ANC in 1944. He replaced J. S. Moroka as president of the ANC in 1952 and, a devout Christian, he fully supported the non-violent protests of the defiance campaign. Nelson was surprised that charges had been dropped against Luthuli and equally surprised that Tambo, twenty years younger than the sixty-year-old ANC leader and well known as one of the party's main organizers, was not to be prosecuted. His release did, however, mean that Tambo could try to concentrate on maintaining their business and ensuring their income.

It was while Tambo was working on a case at their offices that Nelson had what he recalled as an extraordinary experience. He had once had a head-turning moment when he passed a girl in the street who had struck him as being breathtakingly attractive. He had neither spoken to the girl nor even caught her eye but she had made a huge impression on him. Walking into Tambo's office one day, Nelson stopped dead in his tracks when he saw the very same girl, accompanied by a young man, sitting opposite Tambo, clearly new clients. Neslon's friend introduced him to the young man and his sister, Nomzamo Winifred Madikizela, known as Winnie.

Winnie Madikizela had recently qualified as a social worker and was working at Baragwanath Hospital in Soweto. She later stated that it was while working here that she first started to take an active interest in politics, her job revealing to her what she described as, 'the abject poverty under which most people were forced to live, the appalling

'It is said that no one truly knows a nation until one has been inside its jails. A nation should not be judged by how it treats its highest citizens, but its lowest ones.'

NELSON MANDELA

PREVIOUS SPREAD: South African musician Vusi Mahlasela and TV presenter Leanne Manas joined Nelson in Johannesburg when he lent his prison number to the AIDS awareness campaign.
LEFT: Outside the 1957 treason trial, Nelson talks to political activist Ruth First, wife of Joe Slovo, who was later killed by a letter bomb in 1982.

ABOVE: Supporters mob the police bus bringing the accused to trial at the Drill Hall in Johannesburg at the start of the treason trial in 1956.

conditions created by the inequalities of the system'. Winnie, it seemed, was the perfect woman for Nelson.

Winnie came from a large family in Bizana in the Transkei and her Xhosa name, Nomzamo, is roughly translated as 'she who tries hard'. It was Nelson, however, who now tried hard to impress the twenty-year-old social worker. Although eighteen years older

ABOVE: Winnie Mandela gives the clenched fist freedom salute in support of her husband.
RIGHT: Chief Albert John Luthuli, leader of the ANC.

than Winnie, Nelson lost no time in asking her out to lunch on the premise of involving her in helping to organize fundraising for the Treason Trial Defence Fund. Over the ensuing weeks and months, he saw her as often as

he could, more often than not at political gatherings or legal meetings concerning the ongoing trial. Nelson introduced Winnie to his children and, when he and Evelyn divorced in 1958, Nelson and Winnie were married.

Although they had a slightly more elaborate wedding day than he and Evelyn had been able to afford, money was still a problem for Nelson as Mandela & Tambo was not in good shape. Tambo's sterling efforts were not enough to repair the damage that had been done by the treason trial, which was, by the time of the wedding on 14 June 1958, well into its second year. Nelson's banning orders were lifted for six days to give him time to travel to Bizana for the marriage ceremony. The couple were to have two daughters,

THIS SPREAD: Nelson married Nomzamo Winifred Madikizela on 14 June 1958 in the middle of the treason trial and had his bans lifted to allow him to attend the ceremony.

Zenani (born in 1958) and Zindziswa (born in 1960).

In August 1958, with all of the preliminary proceedings exhausted, the actual treason trial began in a converted synagogue in Pretoria, which involved a great deal of travelling and expense for most of the defendants. Over ninety of them had to make a five-hour round trip to attend court sessions, most travelling, as did Nelson, by bus. After a couple of months, the government decided not to proceed with the original prosecution at all, but almost immediately issued a new indictment against thirty of the accused, including Nelson. Crucially, to prove them guilty of treason, the government had to be able to show that the accused planned to use violence to overthrow the state. The trial was to proceed in August 1959 with just thirty of the original 156 in the dock.

Nelson and his co-accused shared a top-rate legal team, as they had done throughout the preliminary stages of the treason trial, and Nelson did not, at this stage, represent himself or any of the others in court. That, however, was to change.

At first, the defence tactics were to prove that they were not mindless attention seekers intent simply on causing trouble. Their first witness was a respected doctor with impeccable qualifications, Dr Wilson Conco, who was also an ANC activist. He was followed by president of the ANC, Chief

LEFT: A crowd begins to gather in the township of Sharpeville on 21 March 1960.

LEFT AND ABOVE: At least 69 protestors were killed when police fired live rounds from Bren machine guns and rifles into the crowd at Sharpeville.

Albert Luthuli, who steadfastly refused to be goaded by the opposition and calmly insisted that the ANC pursued a policy of non-violence. Nelson later commented that the judge 'began to see us not as heedless rabble-rousers but men of worthy ambitions who could help their country if their country would only help them'.

While Chief Luthuli preached non-violence in court, however, the very opposite was happening out on the streets. The ANC had planned a huge protest against the hated 'passes' that black Africans were required to carry. The campaign was to begin at the end of March 1960, leading up to a mass burning of passes in June 1960. But, while Chief Luthuli testified in court, ANC rival the Pan Africanist Congress organized its own anti-pass protest on 21 March. A large crowd of people, estimated to be between 5,000 and 7,000, congregated outside a police station in the Sharpeville township about thirty-five miles from Johannesburg, offering themselves up for arrest for not carrying their passes. There were approximately twenty police officers in the station and, while they clearly could not hope to process the arrests of so many people without long delays, the atmosphere at first was restrained and peaceful.

When the crowd more than doubled, the situation changed. Police reinforcements with armoured cars were called in and the crowd was panicked when the protesters were buzzed by low-flying jet fighters attempting to scatter them. The mood of the protesters turned hostile and when the police fired tear gas, they responded by throwing stones. Then part of the crowd surged forward, tearing down police barriers, and police fired live ammunition into the throng. Sixty-nine protesters were killed, including women and children, and at least 180 were wounded. None of the protesters was known to be armed and many were shot in the back as they tried to run away. The incident came to be known as 'The Sharpeville Massacre'.

Photographs of bodies lying in the street appeared in newspapers internationally. The shootings were condemned by countries all over the world and the United Nations declared that South Africa needed to take steps to achieve racial equality. On 26 March, Chief Luthuli burned his pass publicly in Pretoria, with the cameras of the world's press upon him, and called for a nationwide strike on 28 March in memory of those who had fallen at Sharpeville. On that day, Nelson and other ANC leaders burned their passes, again with hundreds of people and the press looking on. Hundreds of thousands of black Africans stayed at home in the largest mass protest the country had seen. The South African Government declared a state of emergency and imposed martial law.

This was something for which Nelson and the ANC leadership had long been planning. They knew that, as the ANC grew stronger, the

RIGHT: Trucks laden with coffins transport the bodies of the Sharpeville victims to a mass funeral.

government would take ever more stringent measures against them. The day would come when they, like the SACP, would be declared illegal. Outlaws in their own country. It was decided that, if he was eventually acquitted at the treason trial, Nelson would go underground when it was all over. He would go into hiding and organize the ANC campaigns without having to concern himself about his failing business or the restrictions of banning orders. Nelson's friend, Oliver Tambo, was to go one step further and disappear from South Africa altogether. From outside South Africa, Nelson would galvanize international opinion against the apartheid regime and ensure that the freedom struggle in South Africa remained an issue of major concern around the world.

In the early hours of the morning on 30 March, Nelson was woken by a violent hammering at his front door. Only the police would rouse him in such a way at such an hour. He said a brief farewell to Winnie and was bundled off to Newlands Police Station in the bleak and bulldozed wasteland that had once been Sophiatown. Using the powers extended to them by the State of Emergency, the police rounded up every ANC official of any influence. Nelson was held in an outside enclosure with around forty other detainees, packed in so tightly that they had no choice but to stand all night.

There were no facilities for the detainees, they received no food or water for twelve hours and were eventually packed into a tiny concrete cell with no bedding and no proper toilet facilities. Frequent complaints did little to improve their circumstances. Nelson, however, was not to be there for long. Like the others still on trial for treason, he was shipped off to Pretoria.

Because so many of the witnesses, including Chief Luthuli, had been arrested, the trial was swiftly degenerating into a farce. Witnesses could not attend and the defence legal team could not have regular access either to witnesses or to their clients. The defence lawyers advised Nelson and the others that they intended to resign in protest, but Nelson persuaded them that it would be better if they stood down on the instructions of their clients. He and ANC general gecretary Duma Nokwe, who had been one of the founders of the ANC Youth League and who was a gifted lawyer (South Africa's first black advocate), now worked from their prison cells to prepare and present the defence for all of the accused.

The situation lasted for five months until the temporary State of Emergency was lifted and the official defence lawyers could return to do their jobs properly. By then, Nelson was a lawyer without a practice. The firm of Mandela & Tambo had been wound up and Oliver Tambo was working in exile. The ANC, as they had all expected, was now an illegal organization.

In August 1960, Nelson was called to testify and defended himself in court as the

RIGHT: Nelson follows the example of Chief Luthuli and publicly burns his pass 0n 28 March 1960.

prosecution lawyers repeatedly tried to brand him as an anarchic terrorist. He later recalled, 'The state was determined to prove that I was a violence-spouting communist.'

On 23 March 1961, a recess was called and Nelson, with the State of Emergency having been lifted and his most recent banning orders having expired, was able to travel to Pietermaritzburg for the All-in African Conference, where 1,400 delegates from political parties and other organizations all over South Africa braved the wrath of the police to attend a two-day event. At the conference, agreement was reached on a series of demands to be put to the government.

ABOVE: Chief Luthuli was awarded the Nobel Peace Prize in 1961.
TOP RIGHT: Treason trial defendants Robert Resha, Patrick Molaoa and Nelson Mandela arrive in Pretoria by bus from Johannesburg.
BOTTOM RIGHT: Nelson singing the ANC anthem 'Nkosi Sikelel' iAfrika' ('Lord Bless Africa') with supporters outside the treason trial court.

Nelson captured the essence of the moment with his call for a National Convention where South Africans of all creeds and colours could sit down together and agree upon a fair, democratic, non-racial constitution for their country that guaranteed voting rights and equality for all. He was duly elected secretary of the National Action Council and his first

LEFT: Nelson wearing traditional Xhosa costume, which he demanded to be able to wear in court.
RIGHT: Nelson often used a beard as part of his disguise when he went 'underground'.

job was to let the government know what the people wanted. Nelson wrote a letter to Prime Minister Hendrik Verwoerd stating that, if the government did not instigate a forum such as the national convention, the people of South Africa would launch a series of strikes timed to coincide with the forthcoming proclamation of the new Republic of South Africa.

The country was about to cast off its ties to the United Kingdom and the Commonwealth. Queen Elizabeth II would no longer be the Head of State as there was to be a new office of State President of South Africa. This was an ideal time for the country to agree a new, democratic constitution. Verwoerd, a hard-line National Party stalwart often referred to as 'the architect of apartheid', appeared to ignore the letter and Nelson's threats to disrupt the 'Republic Day' celebrations scheduled for 31 May 1961. But the government quietly began a military mobilization that was little short of a preparation for war. Police leave was cancelled and military reservists were placed on standby.

The trial resumed on 29 March and, although the defence had not finished their final arguments, the judge (one of a three-judge panel – there was no jury) announced that a verdict had been reached. In part of his summing up, he stated that, 'On all the evidence presented to this court and on our finding of fact it is impossible for this court to come to the finding that the African National Congress had acquired or adopted a policy to overthrow the state by violence . . .'

After four years and four months, thousands of pages of legal documents and millions of words of evidence and testimony, the government's case had simply collapsed. Nelson and his co-accused were free to go. The packed courtroom was filled with the sound of cheering and, once the defendants had fought their way through the hordes of well-wishers to be with their wives and families, they made their way outside to be greeted by more crowds, applauding and singing.

ABOVE: Songs, celebrations and the ANC 'thumbs up' salute as the treason trial collapses.

For Nelson, there was little time to enjoy his new-found freedom. Having already said goodbye to his children before his appearance at the Pietermaritzburg conference, Nelson barely had time to hug his wife before he was whisked away by his ANC comrades to spend the night at a secret location in Johannesburg. His life as a clandestine ANC operative had begun. He travelled to Port Elizabeth, where the finer points of the structure and organization of the ANC underground movement were discussed. He then moved around from city to city, using assumed names and setting up meetings in safe houses with newspaper editors to let them know that the ANC was still active and that the National Action Council was calling for a convention to discuss a new constitution.

LEFT: Hardline apartheid South African Prime Minister Hendrik Verwoerd with his wife, Betsie. He was assassinated in 1966.
BELOW: Nelson studied the tactics used by revolutionaries like Cuban President Fidel Castro, seen here with him in 1991.

Never staying in one place for too long, he moved from town to town, going wherever he needed to be in his crusade to ensure support for the Republic Day stay-at-home – different from a strike in that there would be no pickets or demonstrations. He stayed in empty flats and safe houses, becoming a creature of the night, lying low by day and attending highly secret meetings in the dead of night.

A warrant had been issued for Nelson's arrest, so anyone found to be harbouring him was also liable for arrest. The police everywhere were on the lookout for him and, once while on the street in Johannesburg in broad daylight, Nelson spotted a black police officer walking

ABOVE AND RIGHT: From being a fugitive in South Africa in the 1960s, Nelson toured the world in the 1990s meeting ordinary people such as the fan for whom he signed a rugby ball in Cardiff, and national leaders like Russia's Boris Yeltsin.

towards him, clearly having recognized him. As the officer drew nearer and Nelson prepared to make a run for it, the policeman gave him a huge smile and brief 'thumbs-up' sign – a gesture that had been adopted as a kind of salute by the ANC – then walked on by. Over the coming years, Nelson was to find that countless black policemen secretly supported the ANC, providing kindnesses to Winnie and Nelson's family as well as advance warning of

police raids, all at great risk to themselves.

Nelson adopted a number of different disguises when he was on the run, posing as a farm labourer, a cook, a gardener or as a chauffeur. Wearing a long dust-coat and chauffeur's cap made it easier for Nelson to travel by car, especially if he had a white accomplice in the back seat acting as his 'master'. He later claimed to find it easier to effect a disguise if 'I did not walk as tall or stand as straight. I spoke more softly with less

clarity and distinction.'

The elusive Mandela was dubbed 'The Black Pimpernel', after *The Scarlet Pimpernel*, a 1903 play and later novel by Baroness Orczy, which was set in 1793 featuring an English nobleman running secret operations in France to spirit French aristocrats out of the country before French revolutionaries could hunt them down and send them to the guillotine. The fictional Englishman, whom the French could never track down, was

known as 'The Scarlet Pimpernel'. Nelson did a great deal to help promote the image of The Black Pimpernel, using public call boxes all over the country to make regular phone calls to the newspapers, reiterating the ANC and National Action Council's demands and belittling the authorities for being unable to apprehend him.

Nelson was able to remain at large, but in the run-up to Republic Day, there were police raids across the country where brutal tactics were used in an effort to suppress any protests against the new republic. Police and army armoured cars patrolled the streets in black areas, sealing them off in a deliberate show of strength. Nevertheless, thousands chose to stay at home on the first day of the protest, 29 May 1961. Half of Johannesburg's workers stayed at home, risking their jobs, and around the country the percentage was even higher. Such was the intimidation and the strength of the military presence, however, that Nelson called off the stay-at-home on the second day. The clampdown by the authorities meant that, on 31 May, the Rolls-Royce limousines swept through the orderly crowds of white supporters bringing Prime Minister Verwoerd and the new President (hard-line apartheid advocate and National Party elder statesman Charles Robberts Swart) to the ceremony in Church Square, Pretoria, unimpeded. The

state was prepared to use threats, violence, brutality, torture and all of its military might against its own people and it was now clear to Nelson that passive resistance was no longer the answer.

Nelson persuaded the national executive of the ANC that the only way forward was to fight force with force and embark on a military campaign. He was tasked with forming a fighting force which was called Umkhonto we Sizwe (MK), meaning 'Spear of the Nation', with himself, Walter Sisulu and Joe Slovo as its high command. The new military arm of the ANC, unlike the ANC itself at that time, did not exclude white South Africans from its ranks. Through Joe Slovo, Nelson was able to call upon the services

LEFT: The United Nations had campaigned against apartheid since its inception in 1946, something for which Nelson thanked UN General Secretary Kofi Annan in 2006. RIGHT: Nelson persuaded the ANC that military action was necessary.

of other SACP members with the kind of military experience and expertise they so badly needed. The communists, who had also decided that the time had come for an armed struggle, were glad to have the might of the ANC on their side.

Working in complete secrecy, reliable men were chosen from within the ranks of the ANC and offered the chance to undergo military training. Nelson Mandela, a man who had never been in uniform and who had no military background, now found himself at the head of an emerging army.

ABOVE: Nelson left South Africa without proper travel documents in 1961. He would not have his first passport until 1990.
RIGHT: In Tanganyika Nelson met with Julius Nyerere, the newly independent country's first president.

On 26 June, Freedom Day, Nelson released a statement to the press, calling once more for a national convention to establish a just constitution. His message stated that 'Only through hardship, sacrifice and militant action can freedom be won. The struggle is my life. I will continue fighting for freedom until the end of my days.' He stopped short of announcing an armed campaign – 'militant' is a very different word frrom 'military' – but the threat was there. And the military build-up was well under way.

Nelson arranged for those MK members with military experience to begin passing on their knowledge of explosives and sabotage techniques while he moved to Liliesleaf Farm in Rivonia on the outskirts of Johannesburg. The farm had been purchased using ANC and SACP money, with a white SACP member as the purported owner. Nelson posed as a 'houseboy' doing odd jobs around the farmhouse supposedly to prepare it for the new owner's arrival. While he was there, the first of the MK soldiers arrived, using the house as a stopping-off point before being smuggled out of the country to China for military training.

Organizing an army takes, time, expertise, political backing and money. Nelson was short of all four. MK operations and sabotage attacks against state installations had already begun. Bombs were planted at power stations and government offices. Their aim at this stage was to create maximum impact without any loss of life. Sadly, the first man to die as the result of MK actions was one of their own. Petrus Molife was killed when a bomb exploded prematurely. Expertise in the form of training, political backing and funding had to come from outside South Africa. Nelson was given the task of travelling to different African states to solicit support.

He was driven across the border into Bechuanaland (now Botswana) from where he was flown to Kasane in the north-east of the country before taking another flight to Mbeya in Tanganyika (now Tanzania). Here, for the first time in his life, Nelson experienced what it was like to be a black man in a free country. He stayed at a hotel where there was no segregation, no separate doors for whites and blacks, where he saw black guests and white guests sitting chatting together. It was a strange feeling, being able to walk wherever he pleased without having constantly to look

over his shoulder.

In the newly independent Tanganyika, Nelson met with Julius Nyerere, the country's first president, then flew on to Ghana, meeting up with Oliver Tambo for the first time in nearly two years. The two old friends attended a conference in Lagos, Nigeria, and both then flew across the continent, to Addis Ababa in Ethiopia, where Nelson was to address another conference of African states. His task was to promote the ANC cause and forge links with political groups in other African countries.

In all of the places that he visited, there was always time for sightseeing and Nelson, who read voraciously every scrap of information he could find about the places he was going to, was just as keen to experience first-hand as much of the history and culture of Africa as he could. He was hugely impressed when he saw, for the first time, a parade of smartly turned-out black soldiers marching in impeccable formation in the Ethiopian town of Debre Zeyit. The parade was in honour of the Emperor Haile Selassie, who built a palace in the town and called it 'Fairfield' after the house he once lived in in Bath, England.

LEFT: The Emperor Haile Selassie met with Nelson in Ethiopia in 1961.
BELOW: Nelson with Oliver Tambo in Addis Ababa, 1962.

The Emperor was in attendance, dressed in a highly decorative uniform, and later, at the conference in Addis Ababa, Nelson was to address the delegates immediately after Haile Selassie.

In Addis, Nelson and Tambo also met with Kenneth Kaunda, future President of Zambia, then they flew on to Egypt along with Robert Resha, another of MK's founder members. Resha was to accompany Nelson on the rest of his journey around Africa. They visited Cairo en route to Tunis, where President Habib Bourguiba promised them training for their men and money to buy arms. Advice, encouragement and support with training and funding were also offered in Sierra Leone, Liberia, Guinea and Senegal, where Nelson was supplied with a diplomatic passport that allowed him to travel on to London.

Throughout his travels, except when he spoke at Addis Ababa or met with foreign dignitaries, Nelson used the name David Motsamayi (who had once been one of his clients), and in London, where the South African security forces had many agents, he was careful to maintain this subterfuge. Through contacts established by Oliver Tambo, who was based in London, Nelson met with newspapermen and politicians such as future Defence Secretary and Chancellor of the Exchequer Denis Healey, explaining the policies of the ANC and MK. Although no funding or other aid could be expected from the UK, British politicians still needed to be made aware that the ANC were sane and reasonable people, not the mindless anarchists that the South African Government made them out to be.

While in London, of course, there was time for a little sightseeing and, on finding the statue of former South African Prime Minister Jan Smuts in Parliament Square, Nelson and Tambo joked that it would be nice to see their statues in such a place one day. Forty-six years later, Nelson would be back in Parliament Square for the unveiling of his statue there.

From London, Nelson headed back to Addis Ababa, where he was scheduled to undertake six months' training in the use of weapons and military tactics. In the end, he had just eight weeks' basic training as his presence was required back in South Africa, where MK's campaign was fast gaining pace.

Nelson's route back into South Africa was via Bechuanaland, from where he drove across the border, posing as chauffeur David Motsamayi with Cecil Williams, a white theatre director and MK member, sitting in the back as his baas, the term black employees were expected to use for their masters. After a brief spell at Lilliesleaf Farm, Nelson set off with Cecil to attend a series of meetings. When they were near Howick, not far from Pietermaritzburg, another car pulled in front of them and, with three more cars behind, they were forced to pull over. The white men in the cars were police officers, jubilant at finally having run The Black Pimpernel to ground.

RIGHT: Nelson's statue in Parliament Square appears to reach out and hug Big Ben's Clock Tower.

Nelson was charged with inciting workers to strike and leaving the country without valid documents and soon found himself back in The Fort in Johannesburg, where, to his surprise, Walter Sisulu was a fellow inmate. Nelson was able to update Sisulu on his recent adventures and, as the two had been arrested almost simultaneously, they suspected that the authorities had acted on information provided by someone close to them.

There was little point in tearing the organization apart with a witch hunt,

ABOVE: Black African women demonstrate on the steps of Johannesburg City Hall, demanding Nelson's release shortly after his arrest in 1962.

LEFT: Winnie Mandela, in traditional Xhosa dress, attends Nelson's trial in Pretoria in October 1962. ABOVE: A prison visit is portrayed in the 2011 opera Mandela Trilogy, with a screen separating Winnie (Philisa Sebeko) and Nelson (Aubrey Lodewyk).

and Winnie was the one who carried that message to the outside world. When she spoke at the opening of the Transvaal Indian Youth Conference, she made it clear that they 'would not waste time looking for evidence as to who betrayed Mandela. Such propaganda is calculated to keep us fighting one another instead of uniting to combat Nationalist oppression.' When Nelson was transferred to Pretoria, Winnie visited twice a week, as often as was permitted, bringing Nelson food and decent clothes to wear. She was also instrumental in establishing the

'Free Mandela' campaign, which began with a demonstration outside the Old Synagogue court house on 15 October 1962 as the preliminary trial proceedings got under way.

Electing to conduct his own defence, Nelson fully realized that the state had all the evidence it needed to convict him (anyone who is known to have delivered a speech in Ethiopia must clearly be guilty of having left South Africa) and probably to send him to prison for several years. It was clear, however, that the state did not have the evidence to bring any charges relating to the activities of MK. His first move was to request the recusal of the magistrate, asking for him to be disqualified on the grounds that he was a white man, working in a judicial system run by white men that was part of a government

run by white men and that he could not be expected to be impartial when officiating at the prosecution of a black man. 'I detest racialism,' he told the court, 'because I regard it as a barbaric thing, whether it comes from a black man or a white man.'

Nelson turned the trial and the courtroom into a political platform from which he could address the government and, via the press, the rest of the world. He enumerated the injustices that the government had perpetrated upon him and the people of South Africa and questioned witnesses in a way that highlighted the villainy of the apartheid regime. This was not a case that

was to drag on for years, months, or even weeks. Ten days after the trial began, Nelson was given the final word in the form of a plea in mitigation. He concluded an hour-long speech by saying that, 'I have done my duty to my people and to South Africa. I have no doubt that posterity will pronounce that I was innocent and that the criminals that should have been brought before this court are the members of the government.' He was sentenced to five years in prison.

He began his sentence at Pretoria Local, where he spent the first few weeks in virtual solitary confinement, locked in a cell twenty-three hours a day. After a while he was

LEFT AND ABOVE: US President Bill Clinton with Nelson on a return visit to Robben Island in 1998.

allowed to mix with other prisoners and he was soon joined by Walter Sisulu, who was on remand prior to his trial but was given parole and, following ANC instructions, then went underground.

In May 1963, Nelson and a small group of other political prisoners were transferred to Robben Island. The island takes its name from the Cape fur seals that Dutch settlers found when they arrived in the area in the middle of the seventeenth century, robben being Dutch for seal. Standing about 4.5 miles offshore in Table Bay, the island was used as a prison by the Dutch and later the British, also serving as a leper colony and quarantine facility. The waters of Table Bay are bitterly cold and as well known for their treacherous currents as they are for their great white sharks, making escape attempts thoroughly inadvisable.

Nelson was put to work sewing mailbags and prison shirts along with the other prisoners. The island was home not only to political prisoners, but also to hundreds of other maximum-security inmates. Even in the most benevolent of penal institutions, throwing a thousand hardened criminals together is bound to create an explosive

atmosphere, simmering with fear and tension. At Robben Island, the aggression of some of the inmates was more than matched by the brutality of the guards, creating sudden flashpoints of violence.

Standing up for himself, and for those around him, with calm dignity, Nelson displayed a mastery of prison rules and regulations that left no one in any doubt that he was a lawyer and would make it his business to ensure that anyone mistreating him was prosecuted to the full extent of the law. He once warned a prison guard who was about to strike him that he would pursue him through every court in the land and that when he was finished the guard would be 'as poor as a church mouse'. The guard backed down. Trouble for Nelson, however, was brewing far from the shores of Robben Island.

On 11 July 1963, the police raided Lilliesleaf Farm and most of the MK leaders were arrested. The police found hundreds of documents at the farm including exercise books filled with notes in Nelson's handwriting covering everything from military training and the tactics of guerrilla warfare as waged by freedom fighters in other countries, to records of discussions Nelson had had with the leaders of the countries he had visited on his foreign odyssey and his diaries covering the time he spent abroad. Worse still, the police seized a typewritten document that set out in detail the

LEFT: The international relations Nelson fostered on his foreign tour in 1961-62 allowed him to act as mediator in talks between Palestinian President Yasser Arafat and his adversaries in 1999.

plans for MK's proposed Operation Mayibuye, identifying the target areas and describing how four groups of MK soldiers would be infiltrated into those areas to carry out sabotage missions and to recruit, arm and train volunteers from local populations.

In retrospect, it may not have been wise to have allowed the farm in Rivonia to develop into a secret ANC and MK headquarters when one police raid led to the arrest of most of their leadership, including the ANC's highest-ranking official, Walter Sisulu. At the farm, the police recovered enough evidence to put the accused on trial for their lives – the prosecution intimated that in this instance they would be seeking the death penalty – charging them with sabotage and conspiracy to overthrow the state. Having learned from the previous treason trial that making a case for treason required far more preparation than simply proving sabotage and conspiracy, the state prosecutors opted for the latter. The ultimate penalty was the same.

Nelson was transferred from Robben Island back to Pretoria to stand trial alongside the others, although two of the defendants, Arthur Goldreich and Harold Wolpe, escaped from their prison cell by bribing a guard. They were then spirited out of South Africa disguised as priests.

The trial of the remaining accused began on 9 October 1963 in the ornate and foreboding surroundings of the Palace of Justice in Pretoria. The presentation of the prosecution case went on for several months and included, among the 173 witnesses, testimony from

ABOVE: *Police hold back the crowds after the accused in the Rivonia trial were found guilty.*

a trained MK saboteur who had become disillusioned with the organization's politics. Nelson's chance to speak came in April 1964 when the defence opened its case. In a voice that was calm but emotional, his speech scattered with brief pauses that allowed him to continue his address for four hours, he read a prepared statement. The world's press were in attendance and the trial had already brought calls for international sanctions against South Africa, so Nelson knew that his words were being heard not only by the courtroom, but by the whole world.

He explained how MK had come about, saying, 'At the beginning of June 1962, after a long and anxious assessment of the South African situation, I and some colleagues came to the conclusion that as violence in this country was inevitable, it would be unrealistic and wrong for African leaders to continue preaching peace and non-violence at a time when the government met our peaceful demands with force. This conclusion was not easily arrived at. It was only when all else had failed, when all channels of peaceful protest had been barred to us, that the decision was made to embark on violent forms of political struggle, and to form Umkhonto we Sizwe.'

Knowing that the United States Government had been pressurizing South Africa not to impose the death penalty; that British MPs had led a protest march through London and the British Government was urging that leniency be shown; that Soviet Premier Leonid Brezhnev had also become involved and that organizations like dock workers' unions around the world were threatening to boycott South African goods, yet expecting no clemency from the South African authorities, Nelson concluded his statement with the words, 'I have fought against white domination, and I have fought against black domination. I have cherished the ideal of a democratic and free society in which all persons will live together in harmony and with equal opportunities. It is an ideal which I hope to live for and to see realized. But, my Lord, if needs be, it is an ideal for which I am prepared to die.'

On 12 June 1964, eight months after the trial had begun, the judge gave his verdict. All but two of the accused were found guilty and sentenced to life imprisonment. From the cheers, singing and chanting of their supporters inside and outside the Palace of Justice, it might have been thought that they had all been set free. Life, rather than death, was a victory of sorts. As convicted felons, Nelson and his fellow prisoners were afforded no time to associate with their families or supporters. They were taken almost immediately to Robben Island where Nelson Mandela became Prisoner 46664 – the 466th inmate to be incarcerated on Robben Island in 1964.

Many believed that international pressure was such that Nelson and the others would be freed before long. They were all wrong.

RIGHT: Winnie Mandela, accompanied by Nelson's mother, Nosekeni Fanny, outside the Supreme Court in Pretoria on 12 June 1964 after Nelson was sentenced to life.

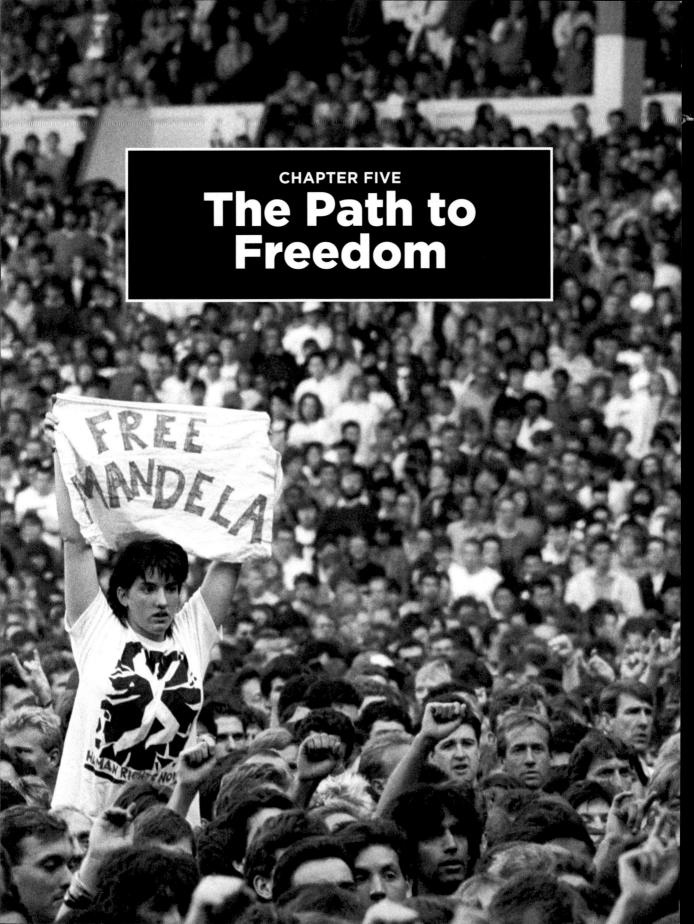

CHAPTER FIVE
The Path to Freedom

The Robben Island experience Nelson had endured for a short spell the previous year was markedly different from the Robben Island on which he now found himself. The authorities had built a new, but basic, cell block solely for the incarceration of political prisoners.

The new part of the prison was a rectangular structure built around a central courtyard of bare, rocky earth. The cells were divided into three blocks and the new arrivals were allocated to Section B, where thirty cells stretched either side of a central corridor. Each prisoner had his own cell, which had a small, barred window that either faced in towards the courtyard or out onto the other compounds and buildings of the surrounding prison facility. On the corridor side was an inner cell door of steel bars and an outer wooden door. The outer door was left open during the day, but locked at night.

The cell was so small that, when he lay down to sleep, Nelson was tall enough to feel the wall at his feet while his head brushed the wall opposite. There was no heating and at night the cells grew so cold, the men having only a thin straw mat on which to sleep and light blankets to cover themselves, that they slept fully clothed. Even then, they had little protection from the chill as the lightweight prison uniforms could not insulate them from the penetrating dampness of their cells.

The prison day began at 5.30am with a warder ringing a bell and the outer cell doors being flung open. The prisoners then had three-quarters of an hour to roll up their sleeping mats and blankets, and tidy their cells before they were allowed out to 'slop out' the buckets they used as toilets. This they did in a bathroom area at the end of the corridor. They were then given a breakfast of cold, watery corn porridge before they were ordered to fall in for inspection. If their cells were not tidy or their uniform buttons undone, they faced a punishment of being deprived of food or locked in solitary confinement.

Following inspection, they were marched out into the courtyard, where they were put to work. Piles of rocks were delivered from the island's quarry each day and Nelson and the others sat in the open air in front of a rock pile, using a hammer to crush the rocks into gravel. No talking was allowed. The prisoners sat and worked in rows, with the white prison guards pacing back and forth to enforce the silence. Even in this bleak place

'There is no easy walk to freedom anywhere, and many of us will have to pass through the valley of the shadow of death again and again before we reach the mountaintop of our desires.'

NELSON MANDELA

PREVIOUS SPREAD: At rock concerts all over the world, young people expressed their support for Nelson, as at this concert in 1988.
LEFT: A guard tower and wall topped with razor wire at Robben Island.

the apartheid system prevailed, for there were no black warders and no white prisoners. Denis Goldberg, the only white defendant convicted during the Rivonia trial, served his sentence in Pretoria.

During the first week, Nelson and the others were told that they had to produce enough gravel to half-fill a huge skip that was dumped in the courtyard. The following week, they had to produce three-quarters of a skipload and the week after they had to fill the skip. In the first of many protests about the conditions in which they were held, Nelson led the Section B contingent in a 'go-slow' to challenge the ever-increasing gravel quota.

Nelson was quick to realize that everything about the prison regime, from the poor-quality food and uniforms to the unnatural

silence rules and lack of proper bedding, was designed to break their spirits and he resolved never to give in to the bullying tactics. In order to do that, however, he needed to make sure that the others were all of one mind and the authorities' biggest mistake was in keeping the ANC men together, even if they could only communicate in stolen whispers. 'It would be hard, if not impossible, for one man alone to resist,' Nelson later stated. 'I do not know that I could have done it had I been alone.'

They worked without a break until a bell sounded at noon and they were served with a lunch of boiled corn seeds. They were then

ordered back to work until 4.00pm when they once again fell in on parade to be counted and marched into the bathroom area. They had half an hour to take a cold seawater shower before another meal of corn porridge and, if they were lucky, a few vegetables were served up. The cooks, inmates from the other part of the prison, invariably held back the best of the food for themselves.

By 8.00pm they were locked back in their cells and ordered to sleep. They had to learn to sleep with the light on as, in the political wing at Robben Island, the light bulb in their cells was left on day and night.

Nelson was categorized as a Band D prisoner, as were the other political prisoners. This was the lowest of four categories. Band

A prisoners were afforded privileges such as being able to receive money sent by relatives. This allowed them to buy, for example, food from the prison tuck shop to supplement their diets. The scale of privileges ranged through Bands B and C to Band D, where prisoners were allowed only one visit every six months. They were also permitted to write and receive just one letter every six months and the letters, both outgoing and incoming, were heavily censored. It could take years of good behaviour to be promoted from one band to the next, and a prisoner could be demoted on the spot for any minor infringement of regulations.

One privilege that was extended to Nelson and the others in Section B after a while, once they had achieved Band C status, was

the right to study. Having study rights, of course, did not mean that all of the prisoners were able to take advantage of the situation. They relied very much on their families in the outside world paying for them to enrol in correspondence courses and paying for the books and stationery that they needed. The prison service provided nothing except permission to stay awake a little later at night to read. Nelson campaigned for months for those who were studying even to have a rudimentary desk in their cells.

LEFT: The courtyard at Robben Island, where inmates were ultimately allowed to mark out a tennis court and tend vegetable patches.
BELOW: Buildings and fences at the Robben Island facility.

Now that they were able to talk among themselves more freely, Nelson and Walter Sisulu gave help and encouragement to those who had the aptitude and the resources to study accountancy or law to achieve qualifications that would be useful in the new South Africa for which they knew their ANC comrades on the outside were still fighting.

News from the outside world came when new prisoners were brought in. Disappointed though he was to see yet another of their number behind bars, Nelson was always eager to debrief MK personnel in order to find out how the struggle was progressing. He learned about the ANC forming alliances and combat troops going into battle alongside other freedom fighters in Angola, Mozambique

ABOVE: Prisoners at work in the courtyard breaking rocks and sewing prison shirts.

and Namibia as well as fighting against South African-backed military units in Rhodesia.

Communications with the outside world were far from easy but coded notes, smuggled out by visiting family members, by lawyers or by departing prisoners who had finished their sentences, all of whom took great personal risks in carrying messages, kept the outside world informed of the conditions on the island. This helped to maintain pressure on the South African authorities, constantly mindful of the stringent sanctions imposed on them by the international community, to improve the lot of Robben Island's inmates. Occasional visits from the International Red Cross, when Nelson was appointed spokesman to air the prisoners' grievances, also slowly led to improvements with better food and more appropriate clothing eventually coming their way.

A new senior officer – the prison was run along military lines and had a commanding officer rather than a governor – was appointed every three years and Nelson made it his business to request an interview with each new incumbent in order to apprise him of the prisoners' ongoing grievances and gauge the best tactics to use in dealing with the new man.

TOP RIGHT: Winnie Mandela at Johannesburg airport in 1985, heading home to Soweto even though she was banned from the area.
BOTTOM RIGHT: Revellers at the 70th birthday party concert for Nelson at Wembley in 1988.
BELOW: Nelson meeting Prince Charles and the Spice Girls in South Africa in 1997.

ABOVE: The stage for the 70th birthday concert at Wembley.

In 1971, one new commanding officer sought to sweep away the reforms that had allowed the political prisoners the opportunities to study and to associate more freely with one another. New guards were brought in, cells were ransacked in searches for contraband, books and letters were confiscated and it seemed as though all of the rights for which Nelson had campaigned so hard were to be denied them once more. Desperate secret messages were smuggled to ANC operatives on the outside, imploring them to highlight the hardships being faced on the island, and Nelson was heartened to see that, even from their prison cells, he and his ANC colleagues were able to bring about change. Within a few months the new commanding officer had been replaced.

If communicating with the outside world was problematic, making contact with prisoners in other parts of the Robben Island complex took even more guile and imagination. The food, however, was generally prepared and served by inmates from the common-law side of the prison and whispered messages were exchanged with those wheeling great urns of porridge into the political wing. A secret note, perhaps hidden in a matchbox, allowed not only for rudimentary communication but also helped Nelson to keep his legal skills well honed. It

RIGHT: Nelson sitting with actor Will Smith and Paul Rodgers, who sang with rock group Queen in 2005. Queen's Brian May and Roger Taylor stand left and right. Nelson had never even heard of most of the performers who campaigned for his freedom and continued to support his causes.

LEFT: Winnie Mandela in 1986 with South African anti-apartheid politician and campaigner Helen Suzman, who visited Nelson in prison.

ABOVE: Nelson with Helen Suzman outside his home in Soweto in 1990.

was expressly forbidden for him to act as legal adviser to any of the common-law prisoners but, using smuggled notes, he managed to help several of them prepare appeals against their sentences. It was a strange experience, working as a lawyer for a client he never saw and was never likely ever to meet.

Some news, however, did not have to filter through from the outside world via clandestine means. Bad news cut through all of the subterfuge. Early in 1968, Nelson received a visit from his eighteen-year-old son, Makgatho, and his fifteen-year-old daughter Makaziwe. He had not seen his children for six years and was filled with pride at how they had grown to become young adults, yet dismayed that he had not been there to watch them do so. With Makgatho and Makaziwe

were Nelson's sister, Mabel, and his mother. He was immediately struck by how careworn and old his mother looked. Because he had four visitors who had travelled all the way across South Africa to see him, Nelson was allowed to spend forty-five minutes with his family instead of the usual half-hour visiting time. The time passed all too quickly, catching up on family matters and news of old friends in the Transkei.

Nelson was summoned to the commanding officer's office a few weeks later where he was handed a telegram from Makgatho, telling him

that Nosekeni Fanny had died. As her first-born child and only son, it was Nelson's duty to arrange for a proper funeral for his mother. He applied for permission to go to the funeral but the commanding officer, with some regret, had to turn him down. While he may have been prepared to accept that Nelson would give his word not to attempt to escape from any escort that was sent to accompany him, the commanding officer could not take the risk that the ANC would kidnap Nelson – albeit against his wishes – and spirit him away.

On 16 July 1969, Nelson was summoned by the commanding officer once again. With a mounting sense of dread he accepted another telegram from Makgatho. Nelson's eldest son, twenty-four-year-old Madeba Thembikele, had been killed in a car crash. Newspaper reports, which Nelson could not see as he was not permitted newspapers at that time, gave the wrong age for Thembi and gave his name as 'Styles Mandele'. It wasn't until later that Nelson discovered that his son was nicknamed 'Styles' because of his stylish dress sense. Nelson's immediate concerns, of course, were for Thembi's family – he had a wife and two small children – and to be able to attend the funeral. He implored the commanding officer to allow him to go to the funeral so that he could fulfil his responsibility as a father to see his son laid to rest. He offered his word that he would not try to escape and said he would forbid any attempts by the ANC to free him but, as before, permission was denied.

Nothing could ease Nelson's heartache at the loss of his mother and his son in the

space of a year, but the prison routine was, as ever, relentless. The hard physical labour had changed from breaking rocks in the courtyard to digging lime at the quarry. Instead of filing out into the courtyard for their morning's work, the political wing were instead loaded onto a truck and driven to the quarry where they were issued with picks and shovels to hack away at the rock face and extract the seams of lime. Just as they had done in the courtyard, they worked in the blazing sunshine and, while their prison shirts and caps kept the sun off their skin, they had no protection for their eyes. Not only were their eyes smarting with the quarry dust that drifted everywhere, coating their clothes and clinging to their bodies, but the sun was reflected off the achingly bright white quarry walls. Nelson petitioned for sunglasses but it took weeks, and a medical officer's warning that the men could go blind without protection, before they were issued with them. Almost everyone who worked at the quarry suffered some long-term effects from the back-breaking work. Nelson worked there for thirteen years, developing a permanent squint and an intolerance for bright lights or camera flashes.

In the outside world, the fight against the apartheid regime continued. Winnie Mandela became heavily involved not only in furthering the cause for black emancipation, but also in turning her husband into a focal point for the struggle. Even as he worked on the quarry face, battling constantly for the most fundamental everyday necessities in prison, Nelson was being hailed as a martyr,

LEFT: On Robben Island, prisoners pooled their rations to create birthday treats. By 1996, Michael Jackson was joining the Mandela family for birthday cake.
BELOW: The lime quarry on Robben Island.

adopted as an icon for freedom. His face was seen on posters at rallies and marches, buildings and streets were named in his honour, songs were written about him and music concerts were staged to keep the 'Free Nelson Mandela' cause foremost in the public consciousness around the world as well as in his own country. Freedom for Nelson Mandela and those jailed alongside him, after all, meant a giant leap forward for the oppressed masses in South Africa.

Winnie payed a high price for her political activities. She was subjected to banning orders, harassed, arrested and imprisoned. Even when she was free to try to visit Nelson on Robben Island, the authorities threw near-insurmountable barriers in her way,

LEFT: *Winnie Mandela speaks at the funeral of a 19- year-old youth murdered by a prison warder in 1985.*
ABOVE: *Winnie with ANC politician Allan Boesak and civil rights campaigner Helen Joseph at a press conference in 1986.*

banning her from travelling by train or car so that she had to take a plane to Cape Town, the most expensive way to make the journey. Winnie never gave up the fight but, as the groundswell of public support for direct action against the apartheid government grew ever more irrepressible, the different factions involved began jostling for power, sometimes turning on each other instead of uniting against the common enemy. Winnie became embroiled in the murky world of internecine politics where the influence of the South African security forces was never far away, encouraging destructive conflict between different groups, always seeking to divide and conquer.

In 1976, when the government ordered that at least half the lessons in black schools should be taught in Afrikaans, students in Soweto took to the streets in protest. As many as 20,000 students headed for a rally at the Orlando Stadium, but along the way confrontations with the police culminated in officers firing shots into the crowd. Famously, thirteen-year-old Hector Pieterson, captured on camera being rushed to a clinic, became the first of at least 176 to die. Details of what became known as the Soweto Uprising reached Nelson via a new breed of political prisoner arriving on the island. Aggressive and unwilling to cooperate with the authorities,

some of these young men had been trained in MK camps and refused to abide by the petty prison regulations. The authorities asked Nelson to persuade them to toe the line in order to avoid the constant confrontations. Nelson declined. 'Their instinct was to confront rather than to cooperate,' he later wrote of the new arrivals. 'The authorities did not know how to handle them and they turned the island upside down.'

The young guns aside, conditions for Nelson and the 'old guard' on Robben Island slowly improved over the years as a result of their persistent negotiating and 'go-slow' work protests. Eventually, manual labour at the quarry was abandoned altogether and the political prisoners were given a far freer rein

ABOVE: Zindzi Mandela with Archbishop Desmond Tutu in Johannesburg in 1985.
TOP RIGHT: Riot police chase a child they said had been throwing stones at them in Cape Town's Guguletu township, 1976.
BOTTOM RIGHT: Apartheid at work in Durban, 1977.

to find constructive means to fill their time. Nelson took up gardening, developing a small plot in the courtyard from which, ironically, he had to dig out piles of rocks to provide his tomatoes, onions and peppers room to grow. As a gesture of thanks for allowing him to grow fresh food, Nelson often offered the pick of his crop to the warders. Nelson put in requests for gardening books and, in general, access to reading material became easier. The political wing was even allowed its

own cinema, with old movies or occasional documentaries projected onto a sheet in the corridor once a week.

Always having been a fitness fanatic, Nelson maintained a regime of exercise in his cell now that he was not forced to undertake hard physical labour. Running on the spot, push-ups and sit-ups helped to keep him in shape and he kept his mind alert by studying. He gained a Bachelor of Laws degree through a correspondence course with the University of London and in 1981 was nominated as chancellor of the university, although in the election he was pipped at the post by Princess Anne. Such was Nelson's popularity that honorary degrees and other awards began to accumulate in his name. He was awarded the Freedom of the City of Glasgow, an honour he greatly appreciated, although he would have preferred to be free in Johannesburg.

In March 1982, Nelson and other senior ANC inmates Walter Sisulu, Andrew Mlangeni and Raymond Mhlaba were suddenly transferred from Robben Island to Pollsmoor Maximum Security Prison on the mainland just outside Cape Town. Another of the 'old-timers', Ahmed Kathrada, followed shortly afterwards. In Pollsmoor they were kept together in a third-floor dormitory where they had proper beds, separate shower and toilet facilities, a separate study area, access to a large balcony and vastly improved food. To Nelson, this was like a luxury hotel compared with Robben Island.

LEFT: *The beach at Durban in 1977, reserved for 'members of the white race group.'*
ABOVE: *Winnie helping to cement relations with Inkatha's Ben Ingubane in 1995.*

Visits, too, were different and progressed at Pollsmoor from the normal maximum security practice of Nelson and Winnie being separated by a barrier, to 'contact' visits where they sat together in a small room. It was the first time that Nelson had been able even to hold Winnie's hand for more than twenty years.

Why he and the others had been moved from Robben Island was not immediately clear to Nelson, although they all suspected that the authorities were worried about the influence that the Rivonia group was having on the new inmates, encouraging them, teaching them and preparing them for the time that they might one day be back on the outside. Another reason, however, was that it was far easier for the government to establish communications with Nelson when he was in Pollsmoor than it was when he was on the island. Nelson had been tentatively offered that chance of freedom on several occasions when he was on Robben Island, the conditions being that he recognized the authority of the government, retired quietly to the Transkei or otherwise bent to the will of the apartheid regime. This, of course, would have meant denying his principles, sacrificing his integrity and destroying any credibility he had as a figurehead of freedom. Nelson steadfastly refused. In Pollsmoor,

Nelson was permitted visits from select foreign diplomats and journalists, approved by the justice ministry and clearly intended to gauge whether his militant attitude had mellowed.

Then, in a statement to the South African Parliament in January 1985, President P. W. Botha offered Nelson his freedom in return for a guarantee that he 'rejected violence as a political weapon'. MK, after a lull in their activities in the 1970s, had embarked on a car bomb campaign against government and military targets that was claiming a great many lives and generating a huge amount of international publicity. The escalating violence, coupled with ongoing international sanctions, was hitting hard at the apartheid regime, causing serious economic problems.

Nelson was seen as part of the solution to those problems.

Nelson's daughter, Zindzi, delivered his response at a United Democratic Front rally in the Jabulani Stadium in Soweto on 10 February. As part of a statement prepared by her father and intended for the people of South Africa more than it was for Mr Botha, she reported that he said, '. . . I am not less life-loving than you are. But I cannot sell my birthright, nor am I prepared to sell the birthright of the people to be free . . . What freedom am I being offered while the organization of the people remains banned? What freedom am I being offered when I may be arrested on a pass offence? . . . What freedom am I being offered when I must ask for permission to live in an urban area?

ABOVE LEFT: Nelson and Winnie with former U.S. Presidential candidate Jesse Jackson and his wife Jacqueline in Soweto in 1990.
ABOVE: Nelson with former South African President P. W. Botha, who offered Nelson his freedom with strings attached in 1985.
RIGHT: Zindzi Mandela rejects Botha's offer on her father's behalf.

. . . Only free men can negotiate. Prisoners cannot enter into contracts . . . I cannot and will not give any undertaking at a time when I and you, the people, are not free.

'Your freedom and mine cannot be separated. I will return.'

Nelson had once again spurned the chance of his own freedom to remain true to his cause. But this time there at least appeared to be a light at the end of the tunnel.

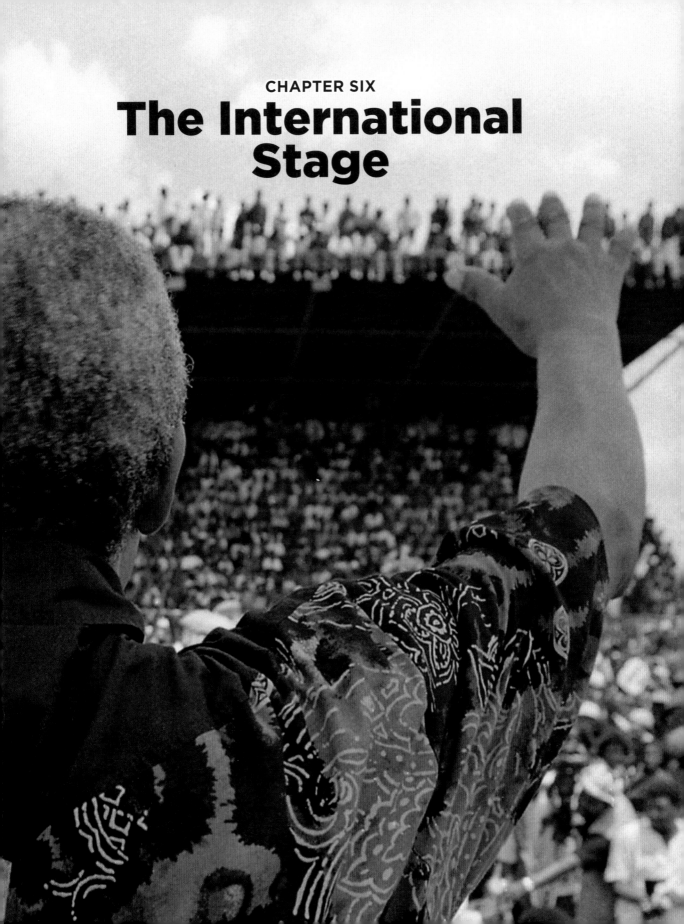

CHAPTER SIX
The International Stage

The conditions under which prisoners in South Africa were incarcerated were not conducive to their leading a particularly healthy lifestyle and Nelson suffered what, for many lesser men, would have been unendurable hardship. His daily fitness regime, once hard labour on Robben Island no longer sapped his energy, helped to keep him in shape, but he suffered a number of health scares nevertheless.

An early prison medical at The Fort in Johannesburg had revealed a problem with high blood pressure, for which he was prescribed medication. Losing track of his dosage and taking too many tablets caused him to black out when in prison in Pretoria in 1963. Following a low-salt diet thereafter helped to stabilize his blood pressure.

Nelson had a number of trips to the hospital while on Robben Island, including one for an ankle injury he sustained while playing tennis on a court the inmates were ultimately allowed to build in the courtyard. Minor surgery resolved the problem but in 1985, while at Pollsmoor, Nelson's health gave far greater cause for concern when he was diagnosed with an enlarged prostate. He was transferred to hospital in Cape Town for surgery where he spent a few days recuperating before being returned to the prison. The return journey, however, ended not in the third-floor accommodation he shared with his friends, but in a three-roomed 'suite' on the ground floor. It became clear that he had been separated from the others in order to make it easier for the government discreetly to maintain some sort of dialogue with Nelson, while also making it easier to limit the number of people who were aware of such discussions. Nelson now had no way of staying in regular contact with Sisulu and the others. The ground floor rooms were also damp, a contributing factor in the tuberculosis from which Nelson suffered three years later.

Talks between Nelson and the government abated, resumed, faltered and restarted a number of times over the late 1980s while the MK bombing campaign continued on the outside, with law courts, military offices, banks and other targets devastated by parcel and car bombs. The government struck back at the ANC, clamping down on sympathisers and suspected organisers inside the country as well as launching cross-border military strikes against ANC bases in neighbouring territories. Despite the violent confrontations happening elsewhere, much of which passed him by completely, Nelson persevered in attempting to negotiate a basis for meaningful talks with

> **'If you want to make peace with your enemy, you have to work with your enemy. Then he becomes your partner.'**
>
> **NELSON MANDELA**

PREVIOUS SPREAD: Nelson greets his supporters at the Ikageng Stadium in the Transvaal city of Potchefstroom during his election campaign in 1994.
LEFT: Nelson walks free from Victor Verster Prison in Cape Town, 1990.

the government. He insisted that, while he had entered into talks with the government of his own accord, he had to be allowed access to his colleagues to make them aware of the situation and win their approval for him to speak on behalf of the ANC. In a move that showed how much the authorities' attitude had changed since the 'no talking' work details on Robben Island in the early 1960s, Nelson was given permission to convene meetings inside Pollsmoor Prison.

Not all of his ANC comrades were in favour of entering into talks with the South African Government, but Nelson persuaded them that an outright military victory was a far-distant dream, while negotiations leading to

the dismantling of apartheid and a democratic system with equal rights for all were very much a reality. He won them over.

Following his convalescence in hospital from TB towards the end of 1988, Nelson was moved from Pollsmoor to Victor Verster Prison, known today as the Drakenstein Correctional Centre, near Paarl, about 35 miles from Cape Town. This was not the high-security confinement that Nelson had been used to. Victor Verster was far less intimidating and he was installed in a cottage with its own garden and swimming pool. Although the cottage garden was surrounded by walls, Nelson was not locked in at night, could get up in the morning at whatever time suited

LEFT: *Nelson and Winnie acknowledge his supporters with the clenched fist black power salute outside Victor Verster Prison, 1990.*
ABOVE: *Nelson's ill health when in prison went virtually unnoticed, but a respiratory problem in 2011 had all of South Africa wishing him well.*

him, swim when he liked and eat when he liked. He even had a personal chef, a warder named Swart, with whom Nelson developed a strong bond of friendship and who 'became like a younger brother to me'. Nelson grew to like the layout and atmosphere in his cottage so much that when he was eventually released, the house he decided to build in his home village of Qunu was virtually identical to his prison cottage.

The cottage had been provided not only to prepare Nelson for his release, but also to allow him to host meetings and to prepare

for talks with government officials. When P. W. Botha resigned in September 1989 after suffering a stroke, South Africa's new President was Frederik W. de Klerk. With de Klerk's cooperation, Nelson was able to secure the government's commitment to the reforms that would end apartheid and bring about majority rule.

Within months of taking office, de Klerk had agreed to revoke the 'banning' of the ANC and more than two dozen other political organizations. It was no longer a crime to be a member of the African National Congress. In October 1989, Sisulu and the Rivonia group were released from prison and in February the following year, it was Nelson's turn. After years of campaigning for his freedom and building him into the personification of their hopes and dreams, Nelson's legions of supporters

were ecstatic at seeing their hero become a free man. His release from Victor Verster was an international media event, with reporters, photographers and TV crews from around the world there to film him walking out of the prison with Winnie by his side. But his arrival at the rally in the Grand Parade outside City Hall in Cape Town was hugely delayed – the car in which he was travelling simply could not get through crowds that swarmed around it.

When he eventually managed to address the crowd, he thanked them profusely for their years of loyal support. 'Your tireless and heroic sacrifices have made it possible for me to be here today,' he said. 'I place the remaining years of my life in your hands.'

Ending the armed struggle against apartheid had not been a condition of Nelson's release and, in fact, he vowed that it would continue. Although he told the world that

ABOVE: Nelson's car was mobbed when he left prison and mobbed pretty much wherever he went thereafter, as it was here on the election campaign trail in 1994.
RIGHT: Nelson and Winnie in the gardens of Archbishop Desmond Tutu's residence in Cape Town the day after his release.

he and the ANC were anxious to achieve a peaceful resolution to his country's problems, Nelson also stated that, 'The factors which necessitated the armed struggle still exist today. We have no option but to continue.' In his heart he longed to return to the Transkei and visit the rolling hills where he had played as a boy, to savour a true taste of freedom and wallow in nostalgia now that he had entered his eighth decade, an obvious temptation to relax and enjoy his autumn years. Yet there could be no relaxing while the cause to which he had devoted his life was so close to achieving its destiny. The danger was that,

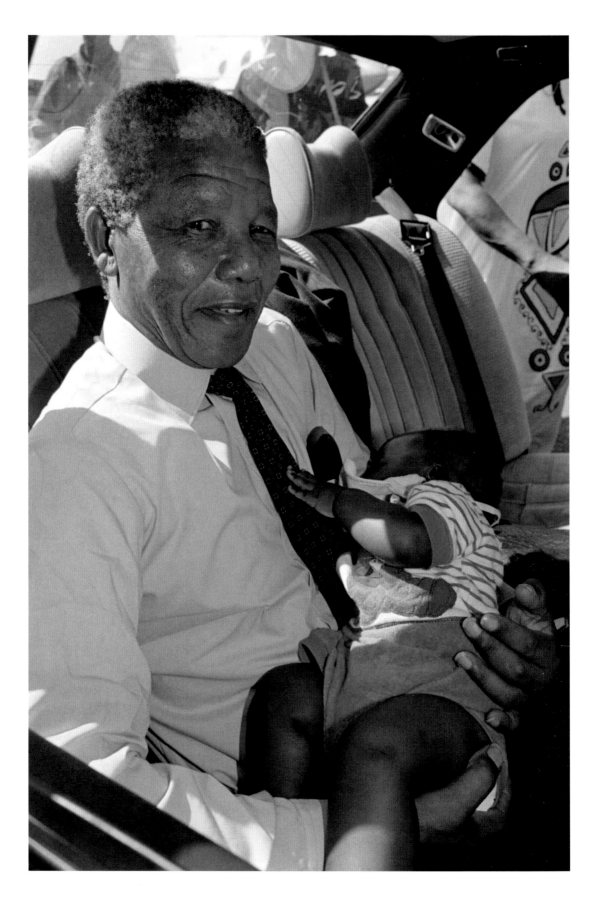

LEFT: Nelson cradles his youngest grandchild, Bambata, in the back of his car the day after he was released.
ABOVE: British Prime Minister Margaret Thatcher urged Nelson to curtail his 1990 tour schedule, but he persevered and became ill with exhaustion.

seeing how South Africa was releasing political prisoners and beginning to repeal the laws that legitimized the deplorable racism of apartheid, the international community would begin to rescind its sanctions. That was not a situation that the anti-apartheid movement could allow. Sanctions had to remain in place if the ANC and other allied organizations were to have the strongest possible bargaining hand at the negotiating table.

Nelson set off on a tour of Africa and was greeted by cheering crowds wherever he went.

In Dar es Salaam in Tanganyika, an estimated half a million people assembled to greet the ANC hero. In Egypt he was able to announce that the ANC was calling a ceasefire, opening the way for further negotiations with the de Klerk government that would eventually lead to free, democratic elections in South Africa. During his first few months of freedom, Nelson also travelled to Europe, the United Kingdom and the United States, discussing the future of his country with the most influential leaders in the world.

At home, however, all was not well. While Nelson and the National Executive Committee of the ANC had ordered a respite in the armed struggle, violent crime in the poorer areas of the country – the ANC heartland – and politically motivated attacks on ANC

supporters threatened to derail the progress towards democracy. On 22 July 1990, heavily armed Zulu Inkatha men attacked ANC supporters in Sebokeng in the Transvaal (now in Gauteng province), using heavy knobkerrie clubs and vicious panga bush knives to beat and hack to death more than two dozen people. The ANC had been tipped off about the attack and had informed the authorities in the hope that the armed men would be prevented from entering the township. The police had done nothing to stop them, nor did they take steps to try to apprehend them. Nelson visited the grieving families, even viewed the bodies in the morgue. He demanded that President de Klerk explain why no official action was taken either to prevent or to investigate the incident, but de Klerk could give him no answer.

Sadly, Sebokeng was not an isolated incident. Especially in the Zulu-dominated areas of Natal, it became clear that elements of the South African police were cooperating with the Inkatha thugs to foment disorder and scupper the ongoing negotiations about the dismantling of apartheid. Nelson held talks with the Inkatha leader, Chief Buthelezi, and, while the two had different ideas about the political future of their country, they agreed that the violence had to end. In fact, the violence continued with rogue groups of ANC youths as much to blame as any other faction.

Winnie was caught up in the turmoil when

LEFT: The bloodshed continued after Nelson's release, as here when cars carrying ANC leaders came under gunfire in 1994.
BELOW: Even on the day Nelson was released there were clashes with the police, in one of which this ANC supporter was injured in Cape Town.

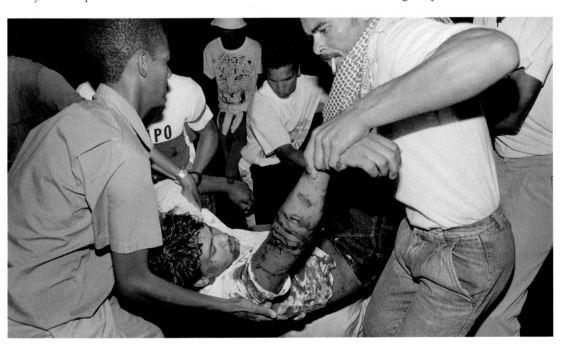

members of the Mandela United Football Club, which acted as her personal bodyguard, were accused of kidnapping, assault and murder. In 1991 she was convicted as an accessory and sentenced to six years in prison, although this was reduced to a fine on appeal.

Nelson made repeated calls for peace but the real solution was to press on with reforming the country. His workload meant that he was fulfilling his promise to his supporters to 'place the remaining years of my life in your hands' but, just as had been the case when he first became involved in politics, he was not able to spend enough time with his wife and family. At a press conference in Johannesburg in April 1992, he announced that he and Winnie were to separate. They divorced in 1996.

Nelson and F. W. de Klerk continued to pursue their course towards reform and were jointly awarded the Nobel Peace Prize in 1993. Nelson was the third black South African to be so honoured, ANC leader Chief Luthuli having been awarded the prize in 1960 and Archbishop Desmond Tutu receiving the award in 1984. Nelson paid gracious tribute to de Klerk in his acceptance speech, the two men

LEFT: Nelson sought peace with Inkatha leader Chief Buthelezi.
ABOVE LEFT: Winnie Mandela at a Truth and Reconciliation Commission hearing in 1997. She had been accused of ordering violent crimes.
ABOVE RIGHT: Winnie Mandela's 'bodyguards' were said to have kidnapped and murdered 14-year-old Stompie Seipei.

standing side by side full in the knowledge that they, with the support of their colleagues, had achieved what many had said was impossible. A date of 27 April 1994 had been set for South Africa's first, free, national elections.

At the age of 75, Nelson was able, for the first time in his life, to cast a vote in an election. He chose to slip his folded voting paper into the ballot box in Inanda, a township just outside Durban in Natal, hoping to demonstrate to the people in that troubled region that it was safe to attend the polling stations. After voting he said that, 'I have fought very firmly against white domination. I have fought very firmly against black domination. I cherish the ideal of a new South Africa where all South Africans are equal.'

The ANC achieved 62% of the votes and on 10 May Nelson was inaugurated as the country's first black president. F. W. de Klerk was his first deputy, with ANC stalwart Thabo Mbeke also serving as Deputy President. In his inauguration speech, Nelson said, 'Let there be justice for all. Let there be peace for all. Let there be work, bread, water and salt

TOP LEFT: Nelson and F. W. de Klerk shared the Nobel Peace Prize in 1993.
BOTTOM LEFT: Violence continued to flare up throughout the 1994 elections campaigns.
ABOVE: At the age of 75, Nelson casts his first ever vote in an election.

for all. Let each know that for each the body, the mind and the soul have been freed to fulfil themselves. Never, never and never again shall it be that this beautiful land will again experience the oppression of one by another and suffer the indignity of being the skunk of the world. Let freedom reign.'

Just over three months later, he made a speech in Parliament thanking all South Africans for showing patience as the new government settled into its role, but adding, 'Yet there are problems that need urgent attention, such as violence in the East Rand and Natal, the wanton killing of security force members, abuse and kidnapping of children and various other crimes. Among these, the traffic in narcotics and drug abuse need the most serious and urgent attention . . . There can be no argument about the need to take urgent, visible and effective measures to eradicate these problems.'

During his term as president, Nelson introduced legislation to tackle a multitude of problems in South Africa, including taking measures to ensure the provision of free health care for children and those in most need;

massive investment in social services and housing with 750,000 new houses built; huge increases in public spending on education with compulsory education for all children between the ages of six and fourteen; free school meals for 5 million schoolchildren; the connection of 3 million people to telephone lines; water and electricity for countless millions of citizens; and a huge catalogue of reforms to laws governing everything from land ownership and industrial relations to child maintenance and disability allowances.

But it wasn't only within his own borders that Nelson was determined to establish South Africa's new image as a modern, forward-thinking nation. He needed to show the rest of the world how much his country had changed. One opportunity came a year into his presidency when, sporting sanctions having been abandoned, South Africa hosted the 1995

TOP LEFT: Nelson meets with Japanese Emperor Akihito and Empress Michiko in Tokyo in 1995.
BOTTOM LEFT: President Mandela with President Clinton, Hilary Clinton and Zindzi Mandela at the White House in October 1994.
BELOW: Nelson with Princess Diana in Cape Town in 1997.

Rugby World Cup. South Africa's national team, the Springboks, once regarded as a whites-only, supremacist symbol of everything for which the apartheid regime was so hated, became the focus of a 'one team, one nation' campaign that saw them improve dramatically on their poor pre-tournament form, winning all of their games and narrowly defeating the All Blacks in the final. Nelson, wearing the same green-and-gold strip as Springboks captain Francois Pienaar, presented the trophy in front of a capacity crowd and millions of worldwide TV viewers at Ellis Park in Johannesburg.

Within Africa, a continent riven with violent conflict, Nelson also promoted unity, calling for Africans to work together to solve Africa's problems. He tried to lend his considerable skills as a negotiator to help resolve disputes such as the wrangles over the Lockerbie trial. Nelson was still in Victor Verster Prison when the Clipper *Maid of the Seas*, a Boeing 747 'jumbo jet', disintegrated in the sky six miles above the small town of Lockerbie in Scotland. The 747 was Pan Am flight 103 from Heathrow to New York and had been deliberately targeted by terrorists who had sent an unaccompanied suitcase by air from Malta to Frankfurt in Germany, then

LEFT: A State Banquet was held in Nelson's honour at Buckingham Palace in 1996 when Zenani accompanied him to meet the Queen and Prince Philip.
RIGHT: In every way, the 1995 Rugby World Cup was an absolute triumph for South Africa.

on to London where it was loaded aboard Pan Am 103. When the suitcase exploded just over half an hour after take-off, all 259 passengers and crew were killed, along with 11 local residents on the ground.

Various groups claimed responsibility for the attack but a three-year investigation eventually led to the indictment of Abdelbaset al-Megrahi, a Libyan intelligence officer who was head of security for Libyan Arab Airlines, and Lamin Khalifah Fhimah, the Libyan Arab Airlines Manager at Luqa Airport in Malta. Libyan President Colonel Muammar al-Gadaffi refused to hand over the two men to face trial and the United Nations imposed stringent sanctions on Libya including the freezing of Libyan assets, the banning of sales of military equipment to Libya, and the banning of any flights into or out of Libya that were not UN-approved.

Nelson, pushing South Africa to centre stage in the international drama and reinforcing his ideal of brotherhood between

nations on the African continent, came to Gadaffi's aid, embarking on a diplomatic mission that was to last for over seven years. Since one of the problems was that the Libyans maintained that the two accused would not receive a fair trial in either the United States or the United Kingdom, Nelson proposed that, in return for the lifting of UN sanctions against Libya, the two men would be handed over for trial in a neutral country. When he became President of South Africa in 1994, Nelson further suggested that the trial should take place in his country.

Although Nelson's proposal met with the approval of President George Bush, Britain's Prime Minister John Major at first rejected the plan. By the time Tony Blair had taken over from John Major in 1997, the plan was evolving

ABOVE: Nelson had tea with one of South Africa's oldest citizens in 2005, 104-year-old Mzamani Ngubeni, saying what a change it made to meet someone 17 years older than himself.
RIGHT: Nelson received a warm welcome from British Prime Minister John Major at 10 Downing Street in 1996.

to hold the trial in the Netherlands, at Camp Zeist, but that the legal proceedings would be convened under Scottish law. Nelson led the negotiations with Gadaffi for the surrender of the two suspects and the men stood trial in the Netherlands in 2000. Fhimah was acquitted in January 2001, but Megrahi was found guilty and sentenced to twenty-seven years. Nelson visited him in Glasgow's Barlinnie prison in June 2002.

Nelson was to serve just one term as

President of South Africa, overseeing the transition to majority rule and establishing the free democratic system of government that he had dreamed of and fought for all of his life. He was succeeded as President in 1999 by Thabo Mbeke. Despite the hectic schedule that he followed throughout his presidency, Nelson still found time to marry again. Graça Machel, twenty-seven years younger than Nelson, was the wife of Mozambican President Samora Machel up to his death in a plane crash in 1986. Graça is a tireless campaigner for the rights of women and children. She was made a Dame of the British Empire in 1997 in recognition of her humanitarian work. When Nelson and Graça married on his eightieth birthday in 1998, Graça became the only woman in the world to have been First Lady of two different countries.

Although Graça encouraged Nelson to try to take on less work once he had stepped down as president, having been involved in politics and social campaigns for most of his adult life Nelson simply could not sit down and do nothing. He established three foundations bearing his name,

the Nelson Mandela Foundation, The Nelson Mandela Children's Fund and The Mandela-Rhodes Foundation. When asked on a radio show in 2001 whether he felt that he deserved a restful retirement, he said, 'I am sure I do. But if there is anything that would kill me, it is to wake up in the morning not knowing what to do. One of the things I believe in is that one should be busy for 24 hours a day. Otherwise I don't think I would have made it to 83 . . . if I was not busy after retirement I do not think that I would have lived as worthwhile a life as I am doing at the present moment.'

GIVE 1 MINUTE OF YOUR LIFE TO AIDS

In July 2001, Nelson suffered the return of prostate problems and underwent a course of radiation treatment. He was not out of action for long, however, and was soon lending his support to the fight against AIDS, something he admitted he had not given a high enough priority when he was in government. He lent his prison number to the 46664 HIV/AIDS awareness campaign in 2003 and spoke at an international AIDS conference in Bangkok in 2004. Nelson was devastated when his son, Makgatho, died of AIDS a year later.

It was around this time that Nelson announced that he was retiring, at least from public life, although he continued to work for organisations that he felt could benefit from his association and advice. One such cause was The Elders. The group was established following a conversation between businessman Richard Branson and musician Peter Gabriel where they discussed how families and villages and other small communities looked to the oldest, most experienced among them for advice. With the modern world 'shrinking' as modern communications reach out even to its farthest flung places, inspiring the description of the world as a 'global village', it could surely benefit from the advice of an impartial group of benevolent 'elders'. Branson put the idea to Nelson and Nelson gave it his wholehearted support. On 18 July 2007, he brought together a council of world leaders that comprised himself, Graça Machel, former

LEFT: Nelson lent his prison number to AIDS awareness in 2004. His son, Makgatho, died from AIDS a year later.

President of Ireland Mary Robinson, former US President Jimmy Carter, former Secretary General of the United Nations Kofi Annan and a number of others, including Archbishop Desmond Tutu as chairperson. Their aim was to help mediate in disputes around the world. Nelson said at the launch of the initiative that, 'The Elders can become a fiercely independent and robust force for good, tackling conflicts and intractable issues. Together we will work to support courage where there is fear, foster agreement where there is conflict and inspire hope where there is despair.' Nelson then immediately took a back seat, becoming an 'Honorary Elder' in order, as he said, to try 'to take my retirement more seriously.'

Over the next few years he did precisely that. Although his voice was occasionally heard, speaking out on issues where he felt he had a contribution to make, he appeared in public only fleetingly. By the time he accepted the tumultuous applause of the crowd at the closing ceremony for the 2010 FIFA World Cup at the Soccer City stadium in Soweto on 11 July, the 92-year-old was looking decidedly frail and from then on reports of his failing health became ever more regular.

In January 2011, Nelson was laid low with a respiratory infection, his lungs perhaps never having fully recovered from the tuberculosis he had contracted in his damp prison cell 23 years earlier. In 1988, it was a disease that might have ended the life of a less robust 70-year-old but Nelson had fought it off, his dreams of freedom for his people and himself almost within his grasp. By 2011, Nelson's legendary fortitude was beginning to fail him and the chest complaint meant spending a few days in hospital before returning home to rest.

In December 2012, Nelson was back in hospital, this time in Pretoria, having again contracted a lung infection but also suffering from gallstones. He spent three weeks undergoing treatment before being released on Boxing Day, remaining under medical supervision at home. In early March 2013 he was re-admitted to hospital for tests, spending just one night, but by 27 March he was back again, this time suffering from pneumonia.

Although he was allowed to return home after 10 days, Nelson's lung condition persisted and on 8 June he was admitted to the Medi-Clinic Heart Hospital in Pretoria. Graça Machel cancelled an engagement in London to remain with her husband. Nelson's eldest daughter, Zenani, flew home from Argentina where she is South Africa's Ambassador, and Nelson's family gathered by his bedside.

Every person will one day roll up and disappear from the earth, but it is my fervent wish that when that day comes, those left behind can say, 'Here lies a man who has done his duty to his country and to other people and to humanity during his lifetime.'

Nelson Mandela, on receiving the Fulbright
Prize for International Understanding, 1993